THE BLACK WIDOW

'a fascinating read with enough juicy details
to keep you hooked'
THE SUNDAY WORLD

'a compelling book' WOMAN'S WAY

'for anyone wishing to have a permanent record of her
extraordinary story, this is the book to have'
THE LEINSTER LEADER

'a good read, cleverly structured ... has all the ingredients
of the murder mystery genre'
WICKLOW TIMES

NIAMH O'CONNOR is a journalist with the *Sunday World*, having previously worked with *Ireland on Sunday* and the *Irish Examiner*. She is the author of several books, including *Cracking Crime: Jim Donovan - Forensic Detective*.

THE BLACK WIDOW

THE CATHERINE NEVIN STORY

NIAMH O'CONNOR

THE O'BRIEN PRESS
DUBLIN

First published 2000 by The O'Brien Press Ltd,
12 Terenure Road East, Rathgar, Dublin 6, Ireland.
Tel: +353 1 4923333; Fax: +353 1 4922777
E-mail: books@obrien.ie
Website: www.obrien.ie
Reprinted 2000 (three times), 2003, 2006, 2009.

ISBN: 978-0-86278-687-8

British Library Cataloguing-in-Publication Data
O'Connor, Niamh
The Black Widow : the Catherine Nevin story
1.Nevin, Catherine 2.Murder - Ireland
3.Trials (Murder) - Ireland
4.Women murderers - Ireland - Biography
5.Murderers - Ireland - Biography
I.Title
364.1'523'092

7 8 9 10
09 10 11 12

Layout, editing, typesetting and design: The O'Brien Press Ltd
Printing: CPI Cox & Wyman

PICTURE CREDITS

ACKNOWLEDGEMENTS

There wouldn't be a book without Brian's patience and pep talks or the support of Eamonn and Sheila. A big and very special thanks to all those who were involved in the investigation and the trial, especially all the colleagues of 'The Equaliser', Jim McCawl – the man who stood up to Catherine Nevin for a decade, despite the repercussions. Thanks also to the 'Black Sheep' on the northside and the White One, now retired, for the information on the Nevins' early years. Thanks to Andy for explaining the Finglas years. Thanks to Dublin's best news editor, Ken Whelan, for his legal expertise.

Thanks to editor Rachel Pierce for acting immediately on the proposal, editor Íde Ni Laoghaire for her endless and fantastic work and editor Marian Broderick for helping to break the backbone. Thanks to Mary Webb for the publicity, which set the pace, and to publisher Michael O'Brien for the break. Thanks to Des Fisher for his insightful editorial observations.

Thanks Gav, for ringing Gerry from Denmark, and Gerry for the advice. Thanks Al, for explaining how to send an e-mail, and Blackie, for the music! Thanks Ireland on Sunday personnel manager, Oonagh 'of course they won't fire you' McMahon; editor Liam Hayes for the time off; and Ashley Balbirnie. Thanks Siobhan Carmody Collins, Sinead O'Connor, Mary Carmody and Amy O'Leary for all the help. Thanks Niamh Hodgins, Fionnuala McCarthy, Ann Dermody and Kathleen Smith for the advice. Thanks Michael Doherty in the Big Issues for applying his knowledge of Irish history. Thanks Eugene Masterson, Niamh Connolly, Paddy Loftus, Bernard Phelan, Mary Dunne and Marc O'Sullivan for helping out with pix. Thanks Noeleen Farrell for making the last-minute phone call and thanks to everyone who hasn't been mentioned for helping to put it together.

CONTENTS

THE MURDER

THE INVESTIGATION AND THE COURT CASE

PROLOGUE

Tom Nevin was conscious for about thirty seconds after he was shot at point-blank range in the kitchen of Jack White's pub in Brittas Bay, County Wicklow, Dr John Harbison reckoned. The post-mortem on the publican's body was conducted at 4.30pm on 19 March 1996.

The State pathologist of more than twenty-one years' experience removed the fifty-four-year-old's shoes, socks, trousers (which had £3.80 in the pocket), a watch, his jacket (a pocket of which was stuck together with a plaster), jumper, shirt, vest and underpants. On the slab in Wicklow mortuary lay a slightly fat, middle-aged man, 6ft $1\frac{3}{4}$ in height, with slightly receding red hair and freckled skin. He had a stye on his right lower eyelid; his front teeth were healthy. There was a $1\frac{1}{2}$in-long hole in the front right-hand side of the dead man's blood-soaked jacket, dark jumper and shirt.

Fresh blood had settled into scrapes which tapered across his chin. Bruises had begun to speckle his shin. The cuts and bruises showed that Tom Nevin had not died instantly; they were consistent with him banging into the high stool he was sitting on when shot, which collapsed under him with the force of the shotgun blast.

However long Tom Nevin had lived after being shot, death was inevitable, Dr Harbison concluded. The cartridge fired had discharged a total of six pellets. There was a single entry wound on the right of the victim's chest, between his fifth and sixth rib, eleven inches below his top right shoulder.

There were four exit wounds around his left shoulder joint, each about one-third of an inch in diameter. Two lumps of lead remained lodged in the body. The trajectory of the shot rose through the dead man from front to back, indicating that the killer had held the gun at hip level and pointed it upwards and to Tom's left.

The phenomenon known as satelliting, which enables pathologists to estimate the distance between the victim and a shotgun cartridge, had not occurred. Satelliting is the cone-like pattern formed by the pellets of a shotgun cartridge after it has been fired. Up to 400 pellets of lead can be packed into a cartridge, and these spread wider apart the further they travel – the centre-point shows the densest concentration. Bullets of this type are intended for hunters, to compensate for the distance between aiming at and hitting a moving target like a flying bird. In Tom Nevin's case, the cartridge held six pellets – ammunition for game, like deer. Each inch in diameter between the pellets correlates to approximately a yard of distance from the point fired and the target. As no satelliting had occurred, Dr Harbison estimated that Tom Nevin was shot from point-blank range. The maximum distance between the dead man and his assassin was two yards. Even the plastic cards packed into the cartridge with the pellets to prevent them from rattling around, which have no penetrative power on impact, had entered Tom Nevin's chest. The killer probably fired from as little as one yard away.

Everything about the injuries revealed that Tom Nevin stood no chance – there hadn't even been time to put his hands in the air. The documents on the bench where he was working, calculating the takings for the weekend, were undisturbed. There was no smearing of his blood on the floor to indicate that his limbs had thrashed around or that he had struggled.

On the counter, beside a metal soup pot, was a glass of Guinness, which was half empty. Although there was a smell of alcohol from the body, Tom Nevin's alcohol/blood levels showed 119mg–100mg, slightly above the legal level for a car driver, but it would have had a minor effect on the deceased, given his size. It was not a quantity that would have affected his reaction time, if he had been given the chance to react. He had consumed two to four pints, or maybe five, over about two hours prior to his death.

The bullet had risen through Tom from front to back. Two smaller wounds, each a quarter-inch long, were found below his back left armpit, in the outer area, fifty-nine inches above his left heel and a fourth exit near his spine, seven and a half inches below his left shoulder. His right lung was lacerated in the middle and upper lobe; the pellets struck the base of his heart, lacerating his right and left atrium, shattering two chambers of his heart. The pellets carried and injured his two main arteries, his pulmonary trunk and aorta, which was severely lacerated but not quite split in two. The exit holes in his left ventricle were caused either by a pellet or a splinter of rib.

There was very little post-mortem staining, which occurs when the heart stops and gravity takes over, pulling the blood downwards, allowing pathologists to estimate the time of death. Instead of circulating, the blood settles in the lowest blood vessels in the body, causing purple patching. In Tom's case it should have settled in his back, but half his body's volume of blood, around four pints, had actually seeped into the cavity in his chest.

Internally, he showed some signs of heart disease but not enough to kill him, and there was some indication of fat infiltration of the liver, though not enough to indicate alcoholism.

Death was due to an acute lack of oxygen arising from the catastrophic drop in blood pressure that would have resulted from the hole in his heart. Dr Harbison said he could not give an exact time of death because the temperature of the kitchen had helped keep the body warm.

All these things considered, the pathologist estimated that Tom Nevin might have had thirty seconds of consciousness before slipping into a coma. His brain would have died after about four minutes when there was no prospect of the heart restarting.

It would have been long enough for him to register what was, most likely, the last thing he saw – the face of his wife, Catherine.

THE PLOT

Reconstruction

THE SOCIAL WORKER

Catherine Scully couldn't tell if June O'Flanagan allowed her into her home in Clontarf, Dublin, more out of surprise or shame. One way or the other, June genuinely believed there was a social worker at her door. It was 1972 and twenty-one-year-old Catherine Scully was putting into practice a principle that she would live by for the next thirty-odd years: if you can convince yourself of something, you can convince anyone else.

Not every hotel receptionist could manage to get a face-to-face interview with the first wife of the man she herself planned to marry – just by dressing officiously, putting a folder under her arm and speaking confidently. But, then, not every hotel receptionist would want to.

Catherine called to June's door because she had met Tom Nevin in Lisdoonvarna, County Clare, and she was consumed with curiosity to see what her rival was like and how she compared with her.

Every now and then, Catherine could see a split-second of doubt flash across June's eyes as she refused to believe that her Tom could have made a third party privy to the lowest point in their lives. But Tom wasn't hers anymore, and since Catherine knew about so many of the things June was trying to put behind her – a husband, an affair, the pending annulment – June had no choice but to believe that he had. Of all the things June had felt after the break-up, the thirty-one-year-old had never felt ashamed before now. If she hadn't still loved Tom Nevin, she might just have picked up the phone and asked him why. But she did still love him, so she left him alone to get on with his life and get over the whole thing.

Still, she found the questions extremely intimate. What had the frequency of their sex life or the contents of Tom's will got to do with expediting an annulment? But every time June wavered or stalled on a question, Catherine simply dropped the name of a priest from Clonliffe College, who she said was handling the paperwork – and that worked, even if June thought social workers existed only in England. She noticed that the young woman was good-looking, handsome rather than pretty – strong-jawed with a steady eye. She oozed confidence, and her clothes and jewellery looked expensive. Still, June felt she stared at her as if they knew each other, and that made June uncomfortable. Did she know her? She couldn't be sure. The questions about her eight years with Tom, their year in England, what had gone wrong, when and with whom, seemed like an interrogation. The woman seemed to be cross-referencing Tom's answers against her own, but as Tom had told the 'social worker' the truth, there was nothing more to tell.

'No,' June confirmed, Tom had never strayed, and 'Yes,' there was no question of a reunion, and 'No,' of course she would never put in a claim on his will. The things she didn't say were too painful to go into. She got the feeling that the social worker was hungry to hear them too. Catherine wanted to know if he had trusted her implicitly, and if her sisters were also suffering because he had been like a brother to them.

When the social worker left, June hoped that the whole business was finally over – things couldn't get any worse – and then she heard that her parents had been paid a visit and similar intrusive questions put to them. It struck her that she would never escape this part of her past and she was right.

The next time June O'Flanagan saw her was twenty-eight years later when the 'social worker' sat in the dock in the Central Criminal Court in Dublin, charged with Tom's murder. The State Prosecutor, Peter Charleton SC, kept asking the woman, whom June now knew to be Catherine Nevin, if she had any qualifications in social work. But only the three of them knew to what he was referring.

June thought that maybe if she had not had so much pride all those years ago, she might have picked up the phone and asked Tom what need there was to get that woman involved.

But now she was in court and she had the opportunity to speak up.

1

TOM AND CATHERINE

Eight months before his murder, Tom Nevin was lying unconscious on his back on the lounge floor in Jack White's Inn. His head was bleeding. The local doctor was crouched over him, slapping his face and calling his name gently but firmly. It was about 7.15am on 10 July 1995. Tom's wife, Catherine, was standing over him too, agitatedly explaining to Jack White's head waitress, Oonagh Doogue, who had been woken by the commotion, that she thought the pub had been broken into and that the raiders had hit Tom, knocking him out cold.

Tom began to come to his senses. The doctor tried to assist him to his feet, but Tom pushed him off, saying: 'Who are you? What are you doing here?' The publican's head was sore, and he was drunk and disorientated. The last thing he wanted was an audience. His wife became animated and asked him: 'Tom, have we been broken into? Did somebody do this to you?' Tom said, 'No, No,' then stumbled to the Gents just down the corridor and locked himself in. It was the only place he could be on his own.

When Garda Martin Kavanagh of Arklow Garda station arrived, Catherine went to inform him of the situation. An ambulance crew had already been despatched to the Gents to try and coax Tom out. Catherine told the guard, who took notes, that her husband was in the habit of drinking all night after work. Garda Kavanagh asked her if she suspected there had been a break-in and if she thought raiders had caused the injury to Tom's head. Catherine said she was satisfied that nobody had broken into the pub and that Tom had cut himself when he had fallen. But her certainty did not tally with what Oonagh Doogue had witnessed minutes before when Catherine appeared not to know if the pub had been broken into or if Tom had been attacked.

The ambulance men managed to get Tom Nevin out of the Gents after about ten minutes of cajoling, and they whisked him away to Loughlinstown Hospital in Dublin for stitches to a nasty head wound.

Three months later, on 12 October 1995, another ambulance crew arrived at Jack White's and this time Catherine took them to Tom's bedroom, where Tom lay in pain. Tom told them that he had fallen and injured his back, but, again, it was never established exactly how this had happened.

Twice in the space of just four months, less than a year before he was murdered on 19 March 1996, Tom Nevin required medical attention for injuries he had procured on the premises, the causes of which were never satisfactorily explained.

Suspicion began to point towards his wife. Her temper was legendary. On 30 August 1991, Garda Mick Murphy, attached to Arklow station, saw her hurl a bottle at her husband during a row. The pub's cleaner, Janey Murphy, who worked there from 1987 to 1996, recalls Catherine pushing Tom down the stairs, on a date unknown, and she states that 'His ribs were very sore for a good while after that.'

Catherine's own step-aunt, Patricia Flood, made two statements to gardaí after Tom's murder in 1996, which she subsequently confirmed in interviews, in which she claimed that Tom was not only 'afraid' of Catherine, but that

Catherine had threatened to have him 'blown away'. In the first statement, Flood claimed that Tom Nevin had visited her over Christmas in 1994:

'Tom was on his own. I cannot recall what the conversation was about, but it must have been about Catherine. He mentioned her to me and he was crying. He put his hands over his face and he started to cry. He said, "You don't know what I have to put up with, you don't know the half of it!" He went on to say, "How would you like to see [Garda Inspector] Tom Kennedy coming out of Catherine's room in the morning?" This shocked me. Tom Nevin then went on to say that Catherine was wining and dining Tom Kennedy to the best and he, Tom Nevin, had to put up with it. I said to him, "Is she trying to drive you mad?" I asked him was there any way out, would you not split the pub half-and-half and get out? Tom didn't seem to think he could. I felt there was more to it. She seemed to have some hold over him. It looked like that. I got the impression that Tom was afraid of Catherine. He seemed to be afraid to talk. For the last five or six years Tom Nevin always visited me on his own. For a few Christmases, there, I always received Christmas cards signed only by Catherine. Tom's name was never on them. However, at Christmas 1995 the family received a card signed Tom and Catherine. The cards were always signed by Catherine. On the 26/27 January 1996 my husband's sister, Mary O'Driscoll, died. Catherine came down for the funeral; Tom Nevin appeared with her. This was the first time the two of them had appeared together in 5/6 years to my knowledge. Looking back on it now, I thought this strange. Last Christmas, 1995 – a couple of days before it – Tom Nevin was in a rush, he called to my house. I asked him how things were between himself and Catherine. He said that the relationship between Tom Kennedy and Catherine seemed to have ended. I asked him if everything was all right and he shrugged his shoulders and said things were just the same. By this I took to mean that the relationship between himself and Catherine was as bad as ever. That Christmas, Tom was very down-and-out. He looked to me to be very depressed. I felt very sorry for him as I felt things weren't right. He seemed to me to be like a man that didn't care.'

Some time later, Patricia Flood came back to the gardaí to make a second statement. This time she said:

'I asked you to come over and talk to me tonight as there is something on my mind that I want to tell you about with regard to Tom Nevin. I didn't say it to you before as Catherine's father wasn't well and I was concerned about Catherine's mother. This has been niggling in my mind and I want to tell you before it is too late. When Tom Nevin called to see me at Christmas '94 he told me more than what I told you in my first statement. He was very upset and crying. He told me that his life was threatened by Catherine Nevin a few times. He told me that she had said to him that she was going to have him blown away. He was afraid for his life. This shocked me and caught me unawares. I said to him, "She doesn't mean it." He said to me, "She means it all right." I asked him, Why doesn't he split the pub in half and get out. He said he couldn't because she wouldn't let him. He said he wanted to get out. He stood up and shook his head and said, "Tricia, you don't know the half of it," and he left. Between Christmas '94 and Christmas '95 – I can't put an exact date on it – he called to see me again, just dropped in for a while. Again he was upset and the conversation came up about Catherine and the pub. He told me that Catherine had threatened him again – to get him blown away. This was the same as he had told me the previous Christmas. I felt he was a broken man. I feel sorry now that I didn't go into it deeper with him at the time. At the time I didn't know how to respond to him. I couldn't believe it. I said to him, "I don't believe Catherine would do that, Tom." He said to me, "You don't know Catherine."'

Tom's own brother, Seán, the youngest of the nine Nevin

siblings and eighteen years Tom's junior, saw his eldest brother regularly. Seán is a carpenter and when collecting ash timber from Wicklow to make hurleys he would call in to see his brother in Jack White's. In late 1994, Seán had a long chat with Tom at their home place in Tynagh, County Galway. Tom spoke about a lot of things, but, unusually, not about his plans. At the time, Seán thought it strange; in retrospect, he believes it was a sign that Tom was not looking forward to the future. 'He called at around 4.30 or five and was not in a rush to go. I think he wanted to stay. He was always talking about his plans, whether it was the fields behind Jack White's he was hoping to buy, or about buying another pub. There was no talk that day.'

The family knew that the couple were estranged. They believed Tom stayed with Catherine because he did not want to put his elderly mother through a second marriage break-up. Tom's first marriage to June O'Flanagan had been annulled after eight years. He did not discuss the state of his second marriage with his family; it was not in his nature to complain about his lot and they felt it was not their business to pry. But it did not go unnoticed by them that he was making more and more frequent trips to the family home in Galway, taking their mother, Nora, off for the day and staying weekends.

Another insight into Tom's state of mind in his final years was given by a man who came to know him in March 1993 when both were patients of St John of God's Hospital, receiving treatment for alcohol addiction. The man describes Tom Nevin as 'quiet'. He went on to tell gardaí: 'Catherine Nevin treated him like a piece of shit. Her only purpose in visiting him was to get him to do the books. She put minimum effort into the contact-care element of treatment. Tom Nevin said he did not have a drink problem and was convinced his wife was trying to get the pub off him. He said anybody could have her but himself.'

✦ ✦ ✦

If the final years of the Nevins' twenty-year marriage were characterised by violence, in the beginning the overriding sentiment was ambition.

Catherine and Tom met in the Castle Hotel in Dublin, according to the account she gave to the jury during her trial for his murder on 14 March 2000, four years to the month after his assassination. But she told staff in Jack White's a different story: that she had met him at the Bachelor Festival in Lisdoonvarna, County Clare, in 1970, when she was just nineteen.

Catherine Scully grew up in Nurney, County Kildare, with a younger sister, Betty, and brother, Vincent, who got polio at the age of two. Their father, Patrick, was a farmer who worked a thirty-acre farm, and their mother, Mary, was a seamstress. Catherine went to Nurney National School and then on to the Presentation College in Kildare town, where she sat her Leaving Certificate in 1969. Following this, she did a course in modelling and deportment in Coleraine, and her first job, at the age of nineteen, was in the Castle Hotel in Dublin, where she worked as a receptionist. She lived at first on the hotel premises, then in a bedsit on Ellesmere Avenue on the North Circular Road. At that time, the hotel had a large Republican clientele, and the young and impressionable Catherine could have encountered Joe Cahill (Provisional IRA) and Cathal Goulding (later Official IRA) at this early stage. She herself was drawn to the Republican ideal, employing as her solicitors the firm Hogan and Lehane, which had a strong nationalist history: founder member Con Lehane was a former member of the IRA army council from the 1940s, a War of Independence man and a hunger striker, who left the IRA to set up a new political movement, Córas Na Poblachta (System of Republicans), which claimed, as a fact rather than an aspiration, that the jurisdiction of the Irish state extended over the Six Counties.

In court, Catherine claimed that she did not start going out with Tom Nevin, ten years her senior, until late 1974. In that year, Tom was granted a civil annulment from his first wife, June O'Flanagan, from Ballina, County Mayo, to whom he had been married for eight years. But two years before the date quoted by Catherine as the beginning of her romance with Tom, she visited Tom's ex-wife posing as a social worker and asked the woman intimate questions about the couple's separation. When asked in court if the break-up of the marriage was Tom's fault, June replied: 'It was entirely my fault.'

On 13 January 1976, Tom Nevin married Catherine Scully – the first woman he went out with after separating from his wife in 1970. His second wedding took place in the Church of St John Latimer in Rome. His second wife, just twenty-five years old, already had big ambitions for her future; on her marriage certificate she entered her profession as 'Teacher'.

The couple moved to the basement of a house at Mayfield Road, Rialto, which Tom owned. The rest of the rooms in the house were rented out as flats. Six months after they were married, Catherine bought a house in her own name on South Circular Road. Nine months later the couple purchased a house on Mountshannon Road in Rialto, a house of seven flats, and later they bought a house in Greenpark, Clondalkin. Tom was now manager of his uncle Willie Frehill's pub in Dolphin's Barn. Unlike Tom's first wife, who worked with Tom in pubs in England, Catherine was uninterested in partaking in the pub business, but unable to get work in her chosen career as a model. Ever resourceful, she set up a modelling school, working out of one of the flats on Mayfield Road, but the business folded. Catherine then started travelling around to schools, giving advice on deportment and interview techniques. If offered a cup of tea during a job interview, she would advise, accept; but if offered a ginger-nut biscuit, decline, as it does not break easily in the mouth.

Even at this stage, Catherine was obsessed by her

appearance. Years later she would tell her lover, Willie McClean, that she had had her womb removed in England before she was married so she would not age prematurely and because she did not want children. Her husband didn't know about the hysterectomy, she claimed. Yet on the morning of the murder, she complained of period pains. Over the years, Catherine would take the cosmetic surgery route on many occasions: she would have an eye-lift, tummy tuck and liposuction. She also had a surgical procedure for varicose veins. She would also undergo a procedure to enhance her sexual pleasure; such operations are still relatively new and include piercing the clitoris with a metal stud.

But in 1984, when Tom and Catherine were just eight years married, such things could not even be considered, let alone afforded. In February of that year, Willie Frehill sold his pub and Tom was out of a job.

Tom had grown up on a farm in Tynagh, County Galway, and left it at the age of sixteen to work in England. It was Tom's dream to own his own pub. He served his apprenticeship in bars in Australia and in England, where he lived with his first wife, June, for a year and a half. They worked together in the Spurs public house, managed by Irishman Liam Garret. They worked hard and didn't go out much – they were saving their money to try and improve their lot when they came home. They were very quiet and appeared to be very solid as a couple. Tom worked in Spurs as head barman. Colleagues remember him as good-humoured and placid. It was unheard of for Tom ever to be provoked into a pub fight, although there were plenty of opportunities. He was not overly ambitious at this stage, he was not a drinker and he appeared to have no interest in politics.

But ten years later, while Tom was still happy-go-lucky, his second wife was hungry for a better life, and after the Dolphin's Barn job fell through, Catherine encouraged Tom to set his sights on something higher than another job as a barman. She reminded him that he would never get a bank loan to buy a pub unless he first proved to the lenders that he was capable of running one himself. So the couple began to look around for a pub lease. Catherine got the tip-off about a place called The Barry House in Finglas from a Republican friend. The pub's chequered history was making it almost impossible to find someone to take on the lease.

The pub had been closed because of a riot that had occurred on 30 April 1983 and caused £10,000 worth of damage. It had only just been refurbished when the Nevins stepped in and offered to take over and attempt to win back custom. They were fully briefed about the situation they were about to take on.

At the time of the riot, the manager of the pub was Raymond Doyle, who was running the pub for a second time; it was only his second day back at work. Doyle had been manager some months earlier, but had left after a disagreement. In his absence, a rowdy crowd whom he had barred had returned. Doyle was brought back in on 29 April to try and restore order. He could see after one day into the job that things were out of control and so the next day, 30 April, he hired a bouncer to keep trouble out. The doorman he hired was called Kevin, he had worked in the Rivermount pub in Finglas south. Later that night, Kevin was joined by another man.

On 30 April 1983 the mood in the pub was aggravated by the return of the manager and by the presence of the bouncers. The main agitator was nineteen-year-old Brian Landers, barred during Doyle's earlier administration but back drinking in the pub in his absence. On the day of the riot, Landers had been drinking wine in a field with some friends when, he claims, one of his mates came up to him with his hands covering a badly burned face. The injured man alleged that a man in a chip shop had thrown grease over him after he had tried to rob him, armed with a gun. He asked Landers to mind his gun while he attended to his injuries. It was a single-barrel, bolt-action, sawn-off shotgun, twenty and two-tenth inches long. Landers took it, and started singing with his friends, 'We will not be moved', referring to the prospect of being barred again from Barry's pub. The group, which was by now hyped up, decided to go to the pub with the weapon. On his own admission to gardaí, Landers claimed he 'just wanted to act the hard man.'

The atmosphere in the pub was already tense. A sing-song had turned into a row with the bouncers, and at around 9.00pm one of them had intervened. Kevin had had a glass thrust in his face. There was another row before closing time.

Because of the confusion, Landers was able to slip in. He stood in the middle of the pub, having just pulled the shotgun out of his trousers, cocked it, looked at it, then tucked it back in under his anorak. Then he got a blow to the back of the head from a customer, and as he fell to the floor the bouncers and the rest of the people in the pub set on him. There were around twenty people fighting with their fists and with iron legs pulled off the pub tables.

As the bouncers struggled with Landers' friends at the door, the mob outside, who had been refused permission to enter, turned nasty. They carried pickaxe handles, and started shouting: 'Burn the bleedin' place down.'

Outside, the mob started to block the exits from the pub. A beige Carina car was pushed into the lounge entrance and set on fire. A green Fiat 124, a blue Hillman Avenger estate and a blue Volkswagen van were also robbed and set on fire at the other exits. The crowd were now chanting: 'Ram it, ram it'; 'Burn them out'; and 'Burn the fucking kip.' One barman, seventy-three-year-old William Harmon, watched in horror as the pub windows literally melted and bent with the heat. Gardaí moved in in riot gear and dispersed the crowd, while units of the fire brigade brought the blaze under control. But it was a near thing. No one died, but the pub was gutted. Brian

Landers was convicted of unlawful possession of a gun. Eight others were also charged in connection with the riot.

Catherine Nevin managed to secure the lease of The Barry House for her husband on the grounds that he had been a barman and had experience in another of Dublin's toughest spots, Dolphin's Barn. She also cited her own previous connections in the Castle Hotel. But when the Nevins moved in, so did the Republicans – with an offer of protection that could not be refused. So that there would be no misunderstanding about who now controlled the place, a paramilitary led a donkey into the pub and tied it to the bar in front of the new landlord, Tom Nevin. He ordered a pint for himself and a pint for his animal friend. Tom served him, and also put a pint in front of the donkey. He knew the score and, anyway, he was only biding his time in this pub. He allowed the Republican newspaper, An Phoblacht, to be sold on the premises and on occasions he paid Republicans to mind the door.

Catherine, too, was anxious that their time in Finglas should not be long-term – unless they were the owners of their own pub. But if her husband's reason was security, her own was snobbery. Later, she would describe Barry's to the Central Criminal Court as a 'pub in the middle of a housing scheme, very much a working-class area.' It was frequented by people with colourful names, such as Nicko, Git, Landy, Rasher, Dido, T-Bone, Jeffo, Mono, Baby and Fitzer. (When Gerry Heapes, who later gave evidence for the State at Catherine's trial, told Catherine Nevin's barrister, Paddy McEntee SC, that he did not know the surnames of Mickser and Redser, two men he talked to about Catherine Nevin's plan to murder Tom, it was greeted with incredulity in the Central Criminal Court!)

Although the Nevins were in Finglas for less than two years, Catherine toyed with the idea of burning the pub to the ground for insurance, but word got back to gardaí and it proved too risky. She kept her ear to the ground, drawn both by the threat of paramilitary force and by the appeal of the underworld as the place in which she was more likely to make her fortune. She even visited the Sinn Féin councillor John Jones, who ran an advice centre. Adjoining this was a TV rental shop, where Jones was in business partnership with Dessie Ellis.

Catherine told Jones she wanted to buy a pub and that she had been recommended by the Sinn Féin offices in Blessington Street or Parnell Street. Jones, who would also be solicited by her to murder Tom some five years later, told the Central Criminal Court during the trial that he had never 'heard the likes of such a recommendation'. But Catherine claimed, in her evidence at the trial, that a meeting actually took place concerning the joint purchase, between Tom Nevin and John Jones, of the Killinarden Inn in Tallaght. Catherine claimed in the course of her evidence that the meeting was attended by her husband and herself, and by some well-known Republicans. She said the plan was that the £100,000 needed would be brought down from the North. She claimed that when the bid to buy the Killinarden Inn fell through because of a disagreement with John Jones, her husband 'was very, very upset'. But in his evidence John Jones denied this meeting ever took place. Financial consultant Pat Russell, who was a former Sinn Féin cumann public relations officer, told gardaí in an interview that he recalled something about the proposed business arrangement and he thought that the deal had fallen through because John Jones's wife was against it.

But subsequently, when cross-examined in court by Paddy McEntee SC, he said he didn't recall saying that the Nevins and John Jones were to go into business.

◆ ◆ ◆

Two years later, by May 1986, however, the Nevins were able to produce £270,000 to purchase Jack White's. They had left behind them the problems of The Barry House, but Catherine had brought with her the connections she had made there, as well as a lawsuit taken by the owners of the pub. But by now the couple's marriage was a sham. Catherine's extramarital affairs while in The Barry House were the subject of much local gossip, and at the time of their move to Brittas Bay her then lover, Willie McClean, helped the couple move their furniture.

She was still attempting to keep herself separate from the pub industry and she kept her interest in pursuing a career in the beauty industry going by opening a hair salon and tanning room in Jack White's. But since there was not much trade, and as she had now moved to what she considered a respectable area, she worked out a role for herself in the pub – looking after the food. Her husband was banished to the bar, and the lounge became her domain.

House rules were written up by Catherine for the young country girls who came to work in the pub, and who had to be accommodated at night because of the long distances to their homes: 'Rooms Kept Tidy – Checked twice a week; No Noise after 1pm – consideration for the people who have to work the next day; No cash or jewellery left lying around; Skirts no more than one and a half inches above the knee.' Yet she herself felt comfortable enough in her surroundings to serve customers in her nightdress or bathrobe in the mornings.

In her new surroundings, Catherine still held on to her belief that she was someone highly connected within the ranks of the IRA. Between 1985 and 1986 there had been an incredible transformation in the Nevins' fortunes. Tom had gone from being a barman to being joint owner of a pub worth over a quarter of a million pounds in the exclusive holiday resort of Brittas Bay. How they came about this change of fortune is a mystery. Had Catherine managed to do a deal with the IRA to launder money?

When Catherine dropped the name of an important IRA

man into a story in 1989, the gardaí began to take her IRA link seriously. She reported that a customer had been taken out of the pub at gunpoint and that the man she named was somehow involved in the abduction. At the time, this man would have been rising up through the ranks of the IRA. His identity would have been known only to Special Branch and the IRA itself. An ordinary publican's wife should definitely not have known who he was. He wielded significant power within the Provos. His brother was Number One in the West Dublin Provisional IRA and ran a protection racket.

Catherine's dropping of this name landed like a bomb-shell in the sleepy holiday town of Brittas. Senior detectives scrambled around to see what they could find. But when they investigated, they concluded that the incident had never happened at all. This didn't matter; the important thing was the name she had dropped.

There was something going on, although nobody was quite sure what it was. At her trial many years later it emerged that there were special files in Garda sources on Catherine Nevin. During the trial Catherine's counsel, Paddy McEntee SC, complained that he had not been furnished with the Special Branch files which related to his client. 'My complaint is that we don't know what we ought to know,' he stated. The State Prosecutor Peter Charleton SC replied: 'I do not appear on behalf of the Garda Síochána ... nor will I ask the Garda Síochána to hand over files which may relate to national security.' Judge Mella Carroll ruled that she would read the contents of the filing cabinet and release any information which was relevant to the trial. The files were handed over. The judge's ruling was that the files were not relevant to the case.

On 30 May 2000, about six weeks after the verdict, Catherine's solicitor, Garret Sheehan, received correspondence from the Revenue Commissioners acting on the instructions of the Director of Public Prosecutions. The document contained a list of pubs which the Garda Anti-Racketeering Unit had under surveillance for IRA links. The Barry House during the Nevins' period was on the list – but Jack White's had been removed from it after investigation.

It could be argued that she had turned tout and was now allowed to continue to launder money for the IRA in return for supplying information to the gardaí. There is a degree of licence afforded to garda agents who pass information to an assigned handler. They are afforded a certain freedom from the law so that they can continue to operate, and they are paid. Catherine's credentials had been established. She obviously had inside information. Local gardaí who would not have been privy to this arrangement resented the special treatment. And Catherine seemed to think herself not only above the law but invincible.

✦　✦　✦

Catherine had a terrible hold over Tom. Even Tom's closest family members describe as 'the million-dollar question' his reason for staying with her, when she quite clearly made his life a misery. All her life, Catherine manipulated other people by wielding information over them – like a weapon. If the same is true of Tom, he might also have feared her connections with some of the most influential people in Wicklow. As a seasoned liar, she could take a grain of truth and spin whatever version of events she desired. It is reasonable to infer that she must have threatened to expose something Tom wanted to stay secret. He himself confided in Catherine's step-aunt, Patricia Flood, who felt he was holding back, that he couldn't sell his half of the business. The question then is: to whom was Tom indebted? Secondly, how could his wife, who plotted for seven years to kill him, be in a position to consider herself above the law?

2

THE WALKING DEAD

When Catherine Nevin had a problem in Dolphin's Barn, she turned to the underworld; when she had a problem in Finglas, she turned to the Republicans. But in Brittas Bay a person's 'pull' depended entirely on their respectability. Once again, she correctly identified where to get it, and, once again, how to manipulate it. This time, she wrapped herself around the arm of the law.

The Nevins moved to Jack White's in May 1986, and Catherine immediately began to seduce custom from the garda force. Whenever a garda came through the door, she would send over one of her 'specials' – a coffee laced with whiskey. There were plates of sandwiches and meals, all with her compliments, for her favourites. Rank-and-file gardaí attached to Arklow, Wicklow and Avoca (aka Ballykissangel) did not need much persuading to adopt the pub as their local. If the drink would start to flow for nothing, as it regularly did, they believed the favour was returned by their booking the venue for Christmas functions, charity gigs and retirement parties. But in Catherine Nevin's case, nothing was ever for nothing. The more the guards came in to socialise off-duty, the more she believed she could do as she liked.

Within a year of the Nevins taking over Jack White's,

senior members of the force were also among her regulars. Accordingly, Catherine's sights shifted up a peg, this time in line with the rank of her customer. The ordinary guards socialising in the pub were soon to learn the awkwardness in having their boss, Inspector Tom Kennedy, on the premises.

In 1987, Catherine reported that cigarettes had been stolen out of one of the pub's machines. Although the value of the theft was minimal, she was extremely rankled at the audacity of the thief, given that Jack White's was by now an established 'garda pub'. Three members of the force were despatched from Arklow to take details from the staff. As usual, Catherine welcomed them with 'specials'. When the guards ordered more drinks, Catherine saw it as an affront to her, personally, that they were not taking the cigarette robbery more seriously. At the first opportunity, she reported them to their senior officer, Inspector Tom Kennedy. As a result, the guards in question were severely reprimanded.

Immediately, the first unofficial garda boycott of the pub began. Catherine couldn't understand it. She hadn't wanted the guards to stop coming in; she had simply wanted to remind them who called the shots. But her tale-telling had caused irreparable damage. The garda trade from Arklow all but ended, save for a handful of regulars. These included Inspector Tom Kennedy, fellow Kerryman Dominic McElligott, who was a sergeant in Avoca, Superintendent Bill 'The Bull' Ryan of Wicklow, and Mick Murphy, who hailed from the nearby Barndarrig, and for whom Jack White's was the nearest pub to home. It would be his head that Catherine wanted served on a plate.

After nine years service as a guard, Mick Murphy (34) had been posted to his home town, Arklow. Despite the ill will his colleagues felt towards Jack White's, he saw no reason to discontinue drinking in a pub that had been his local before the Nevins took over. He became good friends with Tom and Catherine. On the way home on 30 August 1991, Murphy called in for a late drink. If he had been hoping for a relaxing pint, he could not have been further from getting one. He found himself in the middle of a row between Tom and Catherine, at a point when insults weren't the only thing flying: Catherine had just picked up a bottle of whiskey and flung it at her husband. It crashed into several glasses, but not into its target. Murphy took his leave. At 10.30am the following morning, he was summoned to Inspector Kennedy's office and asked to give a statement about the incident. The inspector claimed that Catherine Nevin had told him that she had been assaulted by her husband during a late-night row. Murphy said he hadn't seen Tom assault Catherine, in fact what he saw was the other way around. The exchange left him feeling at the very least uncomfortable, and, like the rest of the guards in Arklow, Mick Murphy decided life would be easier if he stopped going into Jack White's.

Catherine Nevin was unimpressed both by Mick Murphy's refusal to back up her allegation and by his continuing absence from the pub. A regular who asked the landlady why the guard hadn't been around learned exactly how strongly she felt. Catherine became highly incensed, cursing Murphy for not standing by her and backing up her claims of assault. Catherine, in fact, was desperate to get a barring order against her husband, but every time she saw her opportunity, she was thwarted. Tom simply was not a violent man and, despite all her efforts, she could not get anyone to say that he was. In her mind it was the one thing now keeping her from getting the business to herself. Catherine finished off the public tirade against Murphy with the warning: 'You'd better tell him to come back in here or I'll have his uniform.'

Mick Murphy did go back to Jack White's, on Good Friday in 1992, with Garda Peter Smith – but in an official capacity. The men had been despatched to do the rounds of local pubs, to make sure they weren't trading alcohol. They found Jack White's open, an offence in itself, and they reminded Catherine Nevin of such. It was the final straw for Catherine, for whom there was no greater insult than being 'double-crossed' by a friend, and, even worse, by a guard who, as she saw it, owed her. Over the next two years, she would make seven different statements about Garda Mick Murphy to his superiors, each containing several allegations – seventeen in all.

The charges ranged from corruption to sexual assault. Characteristically, they were as colourful as they were loaded. Catherine's first principle when spinning a lie was to find the grain of truth – and because Mick Murphy was a former friend, she had plenty to go on.

But by now she had another reason to change the plot and try to keep Murphy and the rest of his colleagues away from the pub. Catherine's plan to have her husband murdered was now fully germinated and she was soliciting criminals to help her. The last thing she needed was some bright spark snooping about the place. Although they had rejected her, as she saw it, the lower-ranking members of the force, trying to make a name for themselves and looking for promotion, just might stumble upon something suspicious.

But she still wanted to get Murphy. One single theme continuously recurs throughout Catherine Nevin's life. When she could not control something, she destroyed it. Her first statement against Garda Mick Murphy, alleging corruption, was made directly to the Chief Superintendent in Wexford, Pat Crummey, now Assistant Commissioner. Like former Inspector Tom Kennedy, Crummey is a native of Kerry. He was later promoted to one of the highest-ranking posts in the force, answerable only to Commissioner Pat Byrne.

The substance of Catherine's first complaint was that Garda Murphy had accepted a bribe. She claimed to have paid Murphy £1,000 to secure a restaurant certificate for the pub on 16 January 1989. Gardaí, in fact, have nothing to do with the issuing of restaurant certificates, but they can object in court to the granting of one. Catherine alleged that she had paid Murphy in cash on the day she was granted the restaurant certificate. In fact, it was Inspector Tom Kennedy who spoke up for her in court, recommending that she be granted the certificate as she had invested £80,000 in refurbishing the pub's kitchen.

Catherine also claimed that one year later, on 1 October 1989, when the pub licence was up for renewal, she paid Murphy another £1,000. She further alleged that in September 1990, Murphy had sought another £1,000 from her so that no objections would be made to her application in court. Although Catherine had made no complaints to gardaí at the time, she later claimed she had told her friend Inspector Tom Kennedy of the alleged bribes. Murphy denied receiving any bribes.

The Garda Commissioner directed that Catherine Nevin's complaints be investigated and one of the country's top detectives, Superintendent Tom Connolly, based in the Investigations Section in Garda headquarters in Phoenix Park, was put in charge.

On 20 July 1992 the investigation began. Murphy's bank account was checked, but there was nothing to substantiate Catherine's claims of any £1,000 payments. Then, on 21 July 1992, just the second day of the investigation, the most damaging and enduring allegation against Murphy was made. A barmaid in Jack White's claimed she had been sexually assaulted by Garda Murphy in the back of a squad car in the summer of 1990, on a date unknown. The girl was only fifteen at the time of the alleged assault. She claimed that there had been a history of kisses and cuddles between herself and Murphy, but on this particular summer night, she alleged, things got out of hand. She claimed that she went to the yard behind the pub after work, where Murphy had parked the squad car, and asked Murphy could she have 'a spin'. She said she wanted to drive the car around the yard. She stated that she, Mick Murphy and Vincent Whelan, the guard he was on duty with, drove down to Arklow Garda station. Murphy then dropped Whelan home. The girl alleged that on the way back to the pub, Murphy stopped the car and forced her to perform a sexual act. Murphy denies all this.

Although Catherine Nevin was not working in the pub on the night in question, 13 July 1992, she also gave Connolly's team of investigators a statement, claiming that the girl had confided in her, albeit some two years after the alleged incident. Critically, on 24 July 1992, Tom Nevin also gave the investigators a statement, and so did the girl. He said that on the night in question, he rang Arklow Garda station to see if the girl were there as she had disappeared from the pub and nobody knew where she was. Tom claimed that the guard on duty told him that she had just left with Garda Mick Murphy and was on her way back to Jack White's.

Connolly's team of investigators contacted every guard attached to Arklow Garda station. None recalled having this conversation with Tom Nevin. But a barman working in Jack White's on the night made a statement claiming he had heard Tom phone the station. The barman later retracted his statement and Catherine told the investigators that he withdrew it because 'pressure' had been put on him from certain quarters. She also alleged that the girl's family was getting anonymous phone calls warning her not to press charges.

On 29 September 1992, Catherine made a fresh statement in which she claimed that she now recalled the date of the alleged assault on the girl; she fixed the date as the night of 8–9 August 1990. When Connolly's team investigated, they found that the date concurred with the roster for Murphy's and Whelan's hours. Every four weeks a guard was rostered for night duty. Both Murphy and Whelan had been on the beat in the squad car on the night in question. Connolly's team seized Arklow station's diaries to check the rostering. It was the single night of the year when both Murphy and

Whelan had been on duty, in the squad car, together. True to form, Catherine Nevin had produced the little details needed to suggest to the investigators that there was no smoke without fire. The Garda Commissioner suspended Garda Mick Murphy in July 1992, pending the completion of the investigation.

But Catherine wasn't finished, not by a long shot. She concocted further stories stating that a local farmer had been forced to pay Murphy £800 not to tell his wife that their daughter had been found in a compromising position with a man. She also said that two local married women had confided in her that they had separately paid Murphy to stop him telling their husbands that he had found them in cars with other men at night. She alleged that Murphy had had intercourse with a young girl after he had found her with a married man in Woodenbridge. Murphy found these allegations ridiculous. But Catherine persisted. She alleged that the young girl had confided in her, telling her that she hadn't wanted to have sex with Garda Murphy, but that she couldn't afford to pay him the money he was demanding to keep quiet. Catherine never gave any names, saying she could not break confidences. But she had dates. She said that the Woodenbridge incident occurred on the day of the local hunt annual dance. Again, her allegations concurred with Murphy's work pattern. The investigators put pressure on her to persuade the women to come forward independently. Catherine promised to try. She even went so far as to say she was travelling to Dublin to speak with the woman with the sole intention of getting her to come forward. The investigation team had her followed. Catherine Nevin did indeed go to Dublin, but not to meet a woman. The team reported back that the person she met was Inspector Tom Kennedy and they stayed the night in one of her flats on Mountshannon Road.

On 28 September 1992, Catherine Nevin told the investigation team that she had something else she wanted to tell them, but that she could not do so because she didn't want to involve another member of the guards. The investigators pleaded with her to help them root out corruption in the force. She sought advice from her solicitor, then told the team that she had changed her mind and would make a statement. It concerned a pub brawl between a former barman, Larry D'Arcy, and Tom Nevin, which had ended up before the courts. The fight between Tom and D'Arcy occurred on 23 December 1988. Catherine alleged that Garda Murphy had approached her on 24 December and told her he'd 'look after things' – for a price.

The investigators, looking into Catherine's claims, visited Larry D'Arcy. D'Arcy said he went to Arklow Garda station to report having been assaulted by Tom Nevin. But, he claimed, Garda Mick Murphy was on duty at the time and told him that he could see no marks on his body. D'Arcy decided there was no point in pressing criminal charges against Nevin, given Catherine's connections in the area. He decided instead to pursue the matter in the civil courts, and he sued Tom (see Chapter 6).

Catherine claimed that Gardas Murphy and Whelan paid her a visit about the D'Arcy case. Catherine's fantasies had developed further, she claimed that Murphy said to her: 'Now, pay-up time is here. I'm sorry it has to be so much but Whaley [Vincent Whelan] knows as well.' She said that she paid Murphy £1,000 in cash and that she watched him count it in front of Vincent Whelan in the car. The guards were laughing at her, she claimed. Although there were no supporting bank records, her claims seemed to be backed up by Tom Nevin, who also made a statement. Tom Nevin said he had given his wife £1,000 cash to pay off the two guards. Catherine had fixed the time of the men's visit at just after 2.00pm. When the investigators checked the rosters, they discovered that Murphy and Whelan had finished work at 2.00pm. Once again, Catherine's information about the men's shift patterns was right. For the investigators, who also had Tom Nevin's statement, it was enough to make them take her seriously.

On 29 September 1992, Catherine went further. She made a statement, this time to fix the date of an earlier allegation in which she claimed that she too had been sexually assaulted by Garda Mick Murphy! She put the date as 27 August 1991. Her date and time coincided with his roster. She identified and named two persons whom she said she had informed of the assault at the time. She said that on 28 and 29 August she had shown these people the bruises inflicted by Murphy. The investigators interviewed the named parties and they agreed that they had seen bruises which Catherine had claimed were caused by Murphy. She again attempted to back up her story by claiming that she had told Inspector Tom Kennedy about the assault.

In October 1992, Catherine Nevin made another statement. She referred to a conversation she alleged she had had with Murphy at lunchtime during the court hearing of the civil suit being taken by the barman Larry D'Arcy against her husband. Catherine alleged that Murphy had offered to 'swing the case' around in her favour by giving evidence for her. She alleged that he told her how he would do it. She alleged that he said: You know me – if the case is going against you, swear up and lie. She even said that Garda Murphy told her it would cost her 'five big ones', meaning £5,000. She later claimed that he asked her for a further £7,000 as he was down £9,000 that he'd invested in a business in Arklow, which had gone bust. Catherine claimed that Murphy said: What other guard would do for you what I did today – fucking lie for you?' This fiction of Catherine's eventually found its way into an affidavit.

This time the investigators discovered the details they were looking for in the fact that Murphy had actually invested money in a company, but that company was in Bray, County Wicklow. They also found that he had given evidence in court which appeared to back the Nevins' case: Garda Murphy said he had not seen marks on the barman, Larry D'Arcy, when he had called into the station.

Nevin didn't finish there. She claimed that she heard Whelan and Murphy plotting to torch a home for insurance money and implicate a local man in the arson. She was emphatic that a 'miscarriage of justice' had taken place. Such was her ability to concoct stories and appear credible that Garda Mick Murphy was arrested and brought to Naas Garda station for interrogation. His partner, Vincent Whelan, was called in for questioning. The men denied all these claims against them – the file sent to the Director of Public Prosecutions recommended that Murphy be charged with sexual assault and corruption, and Whelan with corruption. The men were confined to desk duties pending a decision from the Director of Public Prosecution's office. Hence their nickname 'The Walking Dead'. They were to wait almost two years before the Director of Public Prosecutions decided not to prefer charges as the principal witness, Catherine Nevin, was unreliable.

Reconstruction

THE WEDDING DRESS

As far as Catherine was concerned, her in-laws always held Seán and Theresa's wedding against her. Seán was Tom's youngest brother; there were eighteen years between them. His wife gave evidence during Catherine's trial for murder. Theresa told the jury that Catherine had told family members that she was upstairs, reading, when the raiders burst into her bedroom – a clear contradiction of her story to gardaí in which she said she was asleep. Catherine put Theresa's attitude down to her wedding in 1983 and the dress she had offered to make.

Seán and Theresa were in Dublin, staying with Tom and Catherine in their basement flat on Mountshannon Road on the weekend they announced their engagement.

Theresa was dying to look at dresses in Dublin, but Catherine would not hear of the new bride-to-be having to buy a dress and insisted on making one herself. Catherine's mother was a seamstress and had passed on her trade.

There were visits from Galway to Dublin for patterns and measurements, but never for fittings. A fortnight before the wedding, the bride was starting to get nervous. She rang to inquire. Catherine seemed to think it a bit rich that she was expected to produce a dress at this stage, and she said so! Did they think Catherine was a skivvy? The big day almost had to be cancelled. Seán Nevin kicked himself for not realising that his brother's wife 'wouldn't work to warm herself'.

The problem with Tom's new wife was that she always had to be the centre of attention, the complete opposite to his last wife. And the thing about June was that everybody loved her, and she made Tom happy. Catherine was different. She never seemed content. Planned weekends when the couple were to stay with a brother or sister in Galway were suddenly abandoned in the middle of the night – after Catherine got it into her head that she had not been 'personally' invited. But it was her performance in the run-up to Seán's wedding that finished her with the Nevins, although they were always civil to her.

Nobody wanted her at the wedding as she had nearly sabotaged it. But if she could simply have come and kept her mouth shut, everyone's life might have been made easier. But, true to form, there was a drama and Catherine was at the centre of it. This time she was refusing to stand in for the wedding photos.

It was a double wedding, and trying to organise photos with everyone in them was difficult. Members of the family approached Catherine, attempting to cajole; other family members talked to her sternly. Catherine seemed equally happy with either approach – as long as she took the attention off the bride. Eventually, one of the Nevin brothers roared, 'Leave her to fuck', and with that Catherine was put back in her box, where she stayed for the day.

Even Tom's mother's seventieth birthday party didn't pass without incident, reminding Tom's eight siblings again, as if they needed to know, just how awkward Tom's second wife was. Patsy, the second-eldest Nevin son, who ran the farm, had booked the meal. Spirits were high and everything went according to plan until Catherine arrived in her fur coat, dripping with jewellery. As usual, she made an entrance, this

44

time insisting that she and Tom would foot the entire bill for the night.

Nobody wanted to be under an obligation to Catherine. They had made an arrangement and the arrangement was that Patsy would pay by cheque and they would work out who owed what later. But Catherine wouldn't hear of it, and in order to get on with the night they agreed with her proposal. There were at least seventeen at the three-course meal; wine flowed for the night; there was a birthday cake at the end. The bill arrived, and Catherine insisted on making a show of examining it. There was an embarrassed silence. The family felt belittled by her exhibition.

She started to rant about something and they established that the fuss was about two pints that Tom's brothers, Noel and Seán, had had at the bar and asked the barman to put on the tab. Catherine started to swear, fucking and blinding, and saying that she would not be taken advantage of. It would be Tom and Catherine's last appearance together at a family function.

The Nevins and Catherine met again at Tom's funeral and then in court, when Catherine was on trial for Tom's murder, and Catherine felt it was obvious that they still 'had it in for her'; if they had, who could blame them. She let them know that the feeling was mutual. She made sure that when they were called to rebut her claims that Tom was in the IRA, her barrister interrogated them about their father's intestacy. She made sure to let the court know how 'bitterly' Tom had felt about signing over his inheritance to Patsy, closest in age to him. The Nevins denied there was any such 'cooling off'. Tom had never had an interest in the farm. Patsy was the farmer among them, and they had all waived their rights willingly. He looked after their mother. But Catherine could tell that Patsy was the most shaken by the claim that 'Tom had been a bit peeved'. Although all the family came religiously to court, odd days had to be missed because of children. But

Patsy was there almost every day. His eyes still fill up when he thinks of Tom keeping a pair of hurling boots in the store in Jack White's. Tom had been a gifted hurler. Even though there was no truth in her claim about animosity regarding Patsy's farm, there didn't have to be, Catherine knew how to hit all of them where it hurt most.

Reconstruction

STRANGERS IN THE NIGHT

When Catherine Nevin heard the knock at the door at 4.20am on 22 April 1995 she could hardly believe her ears. For six years she had been hatching a plot to kill her husband that laid trails of suspicion in every possible direction, except back to her. She had planned everything. She had nagged Tom until he agreed to go in to the St John of God's Hospital to get treatment for alcoholism in March 1993. After his death, his admission to hospital backed up her claim that she was the downtrodden wife of an abusive drunk. In May of 1993 she had persuaded him to reorganise his plans for a holiday alone in the Canaries to include a barman whose plans to go abroad had fallen through at the last minute; after his murder, this covered her claim that Tom was 'a queer', a claim that was denied vehemently by the barman concerned. And she had offset any suspicion being potentially pointed at her. Since 1992, Catherine Nevin had made so many charges of corruption against the Arklow gardaí that any move to bring her in would enable her to claim that they were avenging themselves by stitching her up.

It was her claim that Tom was a member of the IRA that was proving most problematic to set up. But because of Catherine's own known association with Republicans over the years, she had to turn the tables and blame Tom.

If Catherine had learned anything from her association with senior members of the garda force, it was that every story must be corroborated. Thus Catherine made sure that there was a grain of truth at the heart of any lie she spun.

So she had planned this night, 22 April 1995, a year before her husband's murder. It was to be a clandestine meeting for men of Republican persuasion in Jack White's. They arrived in two carloads and she set them up comfortably with Ballygowan water (the IRA frowns on its members drinking alcohol) and ashtrays. She laid her shotgun out before them. She then left the scene to avoid being implicated or involved in any way. Her only contribution was to make sure that the lights of the pub could be seen by traffic passing by.

She waited at a window upstairs for a patrol car to pass. She knew she would not have to wait long since the Arklow gardaí had it in for her, she felt, and now checked Jack White's on a nightly basis. But she had not bargained on a stranded couple.

The pair had been making their way back to Dublin in the middle of the night when their car broke down. They were on their way home from a wedding in Avoca and were tired, cold, and a bit scared; there are stretches along the road linking Dublin and Wexford without any sign of life for miles. They had wound up near Brittas Bay on the N11, and they could see the lights on in a pub they knew to be Jack White's. They started to walk towards the pub to ask if they could use the phone. At 4.20am, they knocked on the front door and a very big man answered with a shotgun under his arm. Sitting on stools at the bar behind him were five other men, neither drinking nor playing poker. They looked like the kind of men a person doesn't want to meet in daylight, let alone in the middle of the night. They looked like they were in the middle of a meeting.

The meeting was rapidly adjourned, having been so easily disrupted by mere passers-by. What if the next time it was the gardaí? The men, obviously, had no inkling of Catherine's plans. They got out of the place fast, perhaps beginning to realise the type of person they were dealing with.

◆　◆　◆

Their reaction reminded Catherine of how easily shocked her customers were when she first moved to Wicklow in May 1986. The mountainy men of the Brittas Bay hinterlands hadn't known what to make of the new proprietor – at first. By day she would swan around in a pure silk, duck-egg blue dressing gown or a flamingo-pink towelling bathrobe. There would be accidental flashes of cleavage and thigh for the customers, and roars of frustration at the staff. On her feet she wore high-heeled slippers with explosions of feathers at the toes.

And by her heels there were supposed to be two pet King Charles spaniels – but they always preferred the comfort and safety of one of the lounge couches. If a customer started to pay attention to the dogs, Catherine would get in on the act by filling a couple of ashtrays for them with Harp or Guinness and feeding them KitKats or a handful of crisps. The locals were horrified. Anyone who had ever run their hands along the creatures' backs knew that their fur was matted and they were miserable. Eventually the health inspector made her get rid of them.

By night she would transform herself into the power-dressing 'Lady of the Manor'. She was a blond-haired, foul-mouthed businesswoman – like something straight out of **Dallas** or **Dynasty.**

Nine years had ticked by, and their first impressions of her had now hardened into stubborn opinions, making her life more complicated than ever. They had warmed to Tom, but were suspicious of her.

3

A HARDENING OF ATTITUDES

A person's rank meant everything to Catherine, except when it came to women – and then it meant nothing. Staff whose job was to clean and who were female saw her at her very worst.

✦ ✦ ✦

Kathleen Stafford took extra care with Tom Nevin's shirts. She washed them by hand, ironed them carefully, sprayed them with starch and then ironed them again. It was her way of repaying him for his kindness.

Kathleen had left Wicklow full of hope a few years before the Nevins arrived in 1986. She came back because she had to. She was pregnant and single, and now she was back, trapped in the small town she thought she'd escaped. Things were worse than ever; unmarried mothers still carried their stigma like a cross. At times she thought she was going to suffocate with shame, but she kept going for her son's sake.

As a measure of independence, she got a cleaning job in the local pub, Jack White's. Her boss, Tom Nevin, often told her there was a job for her in the bar or in the kitchen if she just gave him the word. But she didn't want to work under the gaze of the gossip-mongers and give them an excuse to talk about her, so she told him she preferred to work behind the scenes. Kathleen slipped in early in the mornings, and was gone before most of the staff were up.

On pay-day, she collected her son from school and took him to Jack White's with her in the afternoon. She knew she was an overprotective mother, but she was aware that her little fellow felt that not having a daddy made him different. But Tom Nevin made her life easier. He would hand her the wages, and then hand her son a little square envelope with his own name written on it, the same as hers, with a few pounds inside. It made him feel important, that he was looking after his mam and not the other way around. At least when her son went into Jack White's he felt special. Kathleen appreciated that.

So she ironed Tom Nevin's shirts especially carefully and she thought that maybe Tom Nevin knew it and appreciated it. He was kind in other ways too. He rang her the day Hurricane Charlie ripped across the country and told her not to worry about coming in as he knew she was terrified of thunder and lightning; but she still went in so as not to let him down. It was a Monday, and she always went to Dublin with him on that day and cleaned the flats he had there.

When Kathleen's mother died, Tom Nevin brought bottles of beer and whiskey and sandwiches to her home, and told her he'd cater for forty people in the pub on the day of the funeral. When 140 turned up, he catered for them all. They made a collection to pay him, but Kathleen knew it amounted to nothing like what she owed him. So, instead, she spent the money on a bunch of flowers for his wife, though she knew Catherine was used to much finer things than she could afford.

In her wedding photos, Catherine Nevin carried the most beautiful bunch of red roses Kathleen had ever seen. In her wardrobe hung a £2,000 mink coat that Tom had bought her for her birthday, and in her jewellery box she had exquisite charm bracelets, gold chains with fantastic gems, and rings.

Despite everything Catherine Nevin had, Kathleen thought there was something lacking between herself and Tom. True, they shared a bedroom and Tom still wore his traditional Galway wedding ring, the Claddagh. But where he was quiet and gentle, Catherine was loud, with a tongue like a razor blade – if she had an audience. Although she had expensive clothes, there was something cheap about them too – the slits were too high or the buttons opened too low. Where Tom was a perfectionist who did everything for his customers, Catherine treated them with contempt. Bed and breakfast in Jack White's was a big part of the business in the eighties, but Catherine treated it very casually. She would have staff put cereal out the night before, without covers to keep it fresh. She would leave sheets and pillowcases on beds unwashed after guests left. The guests didn't come back and the bed-and-breakfast trade died.

Tom Nevin might never have taken time off in between working, just to eat, if the rest of the staff hadn't taken over from Kathleen and looked after him each day when she left. They made sure he had a meal a day. It was the only time he switched off. Tom barely drank at all in the early days; traditional music and the Galway GAA team were the only things that seemed to take his mind off work.

For whatever reason, Kathleen became the focus of Catherine Nevin's resentment and Catherine made Kathleen's life hell. It started when Catherine asked Kathleen to come and work full-time. It was something Kathleen couldn't do because she had to look after her son after school.

As soon as Kathleen turned her down, Catherine reported her to the social welfare department – not just to the local branch but to the head civil servant in Dublin. An inspector was sent to investigate whether Kathleen Stafford was earning £6 more than she was entitled to earn per week. Her circumstances were evaluated in her mother's tiny cottage in Barndarrig, on the Dublin side of Jack White's on the N11;

her wealth was estimated; her few assets counted. It was degrading and traumatic. Kathleen had virtually nothing in the first place, and Catherine Nevin had everything a person could want. Kathleen couldn't understand how anyone could be so spiteful. More than anything she wanted to walk out of Jack White's, but Kathleen couldn't afford to give up her job.

It wasn't enough that Catherine had stuck the knife in, now she went about twisting it. Every day for five months, Catherine rang Stafford's house exactly ten minutes after Kathleen had left the pub to make sure she had gone straight home and wasn't on her way to do a 'nixer'. On other days, Catherine would drive up to Stafford's door at night and shove the key to the pub through the letterbox, along with a note ordering Kathleen to be in at 7.00am at the latest the following morning. Kathleen would make sure she was in before 7.00am, although there was never any real need to be in so early.

Once, Kathleen sent her son, then nine years old, to collect her wages and Catherine told the child to 'go home and tell your mammy the man in the social welfare is coming to get her.' It was unforgivable to say that to a young child. He didn't sleep that night. But then, Catherine Nevin had no feeling for children. She would often tell her own nieces and nephews: 'Your uncle Tom is building this pub for you' – then she barred them all.

During the week of Tom's funeral, Kathleen Stafford went into the pub to commiserate with Catherine, although she strongly suspected that Catherine was somehow involved. To her amazement, Catherine was having the carpets shampooed. She explained to Kathleen that Tom had booked the carpet service before he was murdered and she didn't cancel because 'it was what Tom would have wanted.' Kathleen was not impressed. She asked Catherine if she had seen his body – she had it in her head that Catherine must have put Tom's glasses back on his nose after he fell. Catherine said,

'Kathleen, I had to mop up his blood.' It was as if she were wiping out all trace of Tom already; Kathleen thought the woman was as cold as stone.

Kathleen Stafford puts fresh flowers on Tom's grave every time she visits her mother's grave in Barndarrig, less than a mile up the road. One of the three headstones over Tom's grave actually has the word 'murdered' on it, like Catherine's final act of power over him. Kathleen says she does not think Tom Nevin rests in peace: 'I know Tom's not happy there, I know he'll never rest in Barndarrig,' she says.

✦　✦　✦

Eileen Byrne left Wicklow when she was sixteen and didn't come back until she was sixty-two. She spent her whole life working for British Rail. She came back in 1992 to look after her mother who had leukaemia and has since died. But before this, Eileen built a granny flat on to her mother's cottage in Kilbride, four miles from Jack White's, and prepared to settle down.

But it was hard for Eileen. She knew very few people locally as she had missed out on a whole generation; she felt her past might as well have been a million miles away, and even her accent had changed over the years.

Everything was familiar yet strange. She knew the face of the young local guard, Paul Cummiskey, because of his likeness to his father, a guard before him in Brittas Bay. She knew Mosey Kavanagh, who drank in Jack White's, not as a labourer fed and clothed by Tom Nevin, but as a child in the school yard.

Even though she was, strictly speaking, a pensioner, Eileen decided to go back to work so she could become part of a community again. She got herself a bike and a job cleaning in Jack White's, then cycled the eight-mile round trip to and from work in the morning.

Although she felt that Tom Nevin's wife, Catherine,

hadn't a benevolent bone in her body, she couldn't understand why this was so. In the community she had left behind, people didn't have much, but they shared what they had with their neighbours. This is what Eileen was used to. But here was Catherine Nevin, with everything money could buy, yet begrudging people the most basic thing she could give them – their dignity.

Catherine left notes out at night for Eileen Byrne to clean the floor and the men's toilet, to put a new tablet of soap and clean towels in the bathroom, and to vacuum the 'crib' (a recessed area) in the lounge. Eileen felt put down by this: she would have done all these things anyway. It was what she was employed to do. Catherine's notes never ended with 'thanks', and it was always to be done 'first thing'. 'All we're short of here is the click of heels and the Nazi salute,' Eileen commented to Tom Nevin.

Eileen just couldn't work out what made Catherine tick. Every move she made seemed to be calculated, and everybody a pawn in whatever latest game she was playing. 'If she can't use you, you won't survive,' someone explained to Eileen when she stood up to Catherine's abuse. One day, Eileen had just cleaned one of the big mirrors in the lounge – the way Catherine insisted – with a bucket of soapy water and newspapers instead of window cleaner and a cloth. It is not easy for a woman of Eileen Byrne's age to carry a bucket full of soapy water the length of the bar, but she is a proud woman and would not give Catherine an excuse to criticise her.

On this particular day, Eileen was just about to go home when Catherine roared out the front door, in front of customers, 'Eileen, what about my mirrors?' Eileen said, 'Catherine, you saw me clean them.' Catherine said, 'I can see marks,' and Eileen felt this was more for the benefit of the customers than anything else. Catherine was talking about five marks scratched along the bottom of the wooden frame by a child with a coin. No cloth would ever get rid of them. Eileen said,

'They're coin marks, Catherine.' She was embarrassed because people looked up to see what was going on. But Catherine said, 'I know my mirrors.'

So Eileen Byrne went back into the kitchen, filled another bucket with soapy water, hauled it the length of the pub again and slopped it down in front of Catherine. She then said, 'Well, Catherine, if you know your mirrors, you'd better sort them out,' and she stormed out of the pub. Eileen didn't last long in her new job, despite her intentions of getting to know her neighbours.

Ironically, it wasn't until she was called to give evidence at Catherine's trial that she really got to know them. Eileen was called to tell what she knew about which of Catherine's 'friends' had stayed overnight, and she had to travel frequently with the staff on the special bus up and down from the Central Criminal Court in Dublin, in case they were called. Finally, Eileen felt like one of them.

When it came to her turn, she was petrified of taking the stand. She had seen Catherine Nevin's barrister, Paddy McEntee SC, make young Jessica Hunter do a complete U-turn on her story about Catherine's behaviour on the night of the murder. Jessica had practically fallen into Eileen's arms when she ran from the dock, sobbing.

When she gave evidence, Eileen answered the questions as succinctly as she could, but she really wanted to tell the jury what was actually going on, like the time she had heard Catherine Nevin say about Gardas Mick Murphy and Vincent Whelan that she had friends in high places and she would see that they never worked again.

Eileen Byrne was in court to hear Catherine give evidence. She thought that maybe if she watched her on the stand she might finally understand what made her tick. She saw Catherine reach into her left pocket with her right hand, and slowly and deliberately take out a folded tissue with which she daintily dabbed a dry eye. Eileen wanted to shout from the balcony not to fall for the act of 'composed graciousness', that this was the woman who shouted 'Don't forget the condoms' to girls of fourteen and fifteen when they were heading off to a disco.

In an interview after the trial, Eileen said that when she heard Catherine claim in court that she had never committed adultery, Eileen wanted to tell them otherwise. She said that when she herself had told the jury that the pub was like Tom Kennedy's second home she was being kind. But it was when she heard Catherine say Tom Nevin was an alcoholic that she most wanted to leap off the balcony and roar 'Lies'. Working on the subways, Eileen had seen enough of winos and alcos to know that Tom Nevin wasn't one. He came down for work looking like a new pin, he was never shaking, his eyes never puffy and he wasn't sweating. Tom Nevin was not an alcoholic. If anything, Catherine was.

✦　✦　✦

Janey Murphy has lived in Redcross all her life and had cleaned in Jack White's from 1987. She nearly left the pub for good on numerous occasions because Catherine had 'vexed' her so much. The reason for the pub's huge turnover of staff was because of the way Catherine treated people, Janey said.

Catherine once put a young girl from Wicklow, who worked in the pub, out on the street at midnight and told her she could find somewhere else to stay. Another time, she made Raymond O'Neill, a barman, keep his shoe on after he had scalded his foot, even though his foot was swollen, because she didn't want customers seeing him in a sock, and she wouldn't let him go home. 'She wouldn't even give him an aspirin for the pain,' Janey said.

She treated her husband equally badly, according to Janey. One time when the couple were supposed to be going away on a continental holiday together, Catherine couldn't find the passports. In an interview, Janey said, 'Tom had hidden them in his own locker.' 'He didn't want to go away with her at all. She called him an "ould fucker" and every name under the sun for hiding them, and he had to go. That was it.'

Catherine, at one stage, imagined she was pregnant, although she had already told Willie McClean that she had had a hysterectomy. It was Janey whom she asked to rear the 'baby'. Catherine would have been dangerous with children, according to Janey. 'She'd pick them up by the scruff of the neck if they came through the doors of the kitchen,' she said.

✦ ✦ ✦

There was a class of people whom Catherine treated even worse than the women who cleaned for her, and that was Protestants. It cost £350 for the Arklow Cricket Club to reserve a part of Jack White's for their prize-giving in October 1994. That covered the cost of a meal for twenty-two and secured the party a bar extension.

The club members laid out on navy velvet their specially polished antique silver, including the trophies and plaques dating back to the former glories of Charles Stewart Parnell from nearby Avondale. Spirits were too high to be dampened by Catherine Nevin coming over during the speeches and warning them to keep it down. Nobody cared when the meal – partly frozen chicken, soggy chips, burnt onion rings and sour corn on the cob – turned out to be terrible. And when an end to the clapping and sing-song was insisted on, the club members obliged because the mood was still good. But when, at 11.45pm, Catherine informed the party that they would have to leave, they asked why.

Catherine announced that the noise levels were 'disturbing her customers'. There was only a handful left at this stage. The club captain, being fair-minded and having regard for the distances members had travelled, intervened. 'Mrs Nevin, aren't your customers only able to drink at this hour because of the extension we secured in the first place?' he asked.

Catherine ordered them out there and then. One member's wife, who had recently completed a catering course, then decided to tell Catherine exactly what she thought of the meal. 'It was as if she had plugged Catherine in,' said Attracta Manson, a qualified nurse, in an interview with the author. Attracta and her husband, Andrew, own the exclusive Ballyrogan Tourist Centre, a guest house situated just yards from Jack White's. 'She started spitting the foulest obscenities you have ever heard come out the mouth of a woman. Her head was bobbing sideways and there was dribble coming out the corner of her mouth.'

After twenty minutes arguing, Catherine had worked herself up into quite a state. 'I am not qualified to make a clinical diagnosis, but she struck me as psychotic,' Attracta Manson said. 'Afterwards, whenever I saw her or heard stories about the latest craziest thing she had done, I thought she had all the characteristics of a sociopath – someone who has to be the centre of attention, whether it's negative or positive.'

The cricket captain responded with the only appropriate words he could think of: 'You're only an oul' cow.'

'And Catherine took the navy velvet cloth in her two hands, carried the bundle of antique silver to the front door and pegged it out onto the N11 in the freezing cold,' said Andrew Manson, an Englishman and husband of Attracta, who was no longer capable of being surprised by his local landlady's behaviour.

Catherine had previously barred Andrew Manson from the pub because of his religion. But he kept going back on principle. 'It's an English thing. Your local is your local. Why should you have to drive for another five miles to the next pub? A chap should be able to have a glass of beer after a day's work, in his local, without having to put up with the ravings of a loony. It used to be a non-sectarian pub before she came along, but she absolutely hated Protestants; they used to drink there no problem, but she got rid of them.' Sometimes Andrew was let in and sometimes he wasn't. One time he asked Tom if he were still barred, but Tom said he'd have to speak to Catherine. 'They had an awful hold over each other,' Manson said.

The Manson's business, Ballyrogan House, was once a health farm and is now a tourist centre. It is a rambling country house with converted stables offering self-catering guest accommodation. Jack White's is the nearest restaurant to the pub, less than half a mile away. When the Nevins first took over Jack White's, the Mansons continued to recommend it as a restaurant to their guests, who mostly came from England and Germany.

'We thought she would have the foresight to know, from a purely professional point of view, that if she looked after our guests, just in terms of being polite, we would sustain the trade to her. But quiet English couples would come back to us with stories about how they had gone in and ordered one thing and she served them something else, refusing to change it.' Then some guests who visited Jack White's got food poisoning, and the Mansons did not mention the place again. 'She was literally hanging dishcloths up to dry in the toilets of the pub,' Attracta said.

In the summer of 1995 Catherine was at her worst, according to the Mansons. 'It was the really hot summer and men were going in sitting at the bar in just a pair of shorts, which she had no problem with. But when this good-looking young woman came in wearing a tight top, she barred the whole pub. There must have been sixty people in there at the time, people who were arriving dehydrated from the beach, being sent away.' There was another incident that year when Catherine barred a busload of forty-five Dubliners who stopped off for refreshments – because they were from Dublin!

She had turned so many people away that it was becoming

a joke. On a November night in 1995, Inspector Tom Kennedy, who was drinking in Lil Doyle's pub, was asked: 'Are you barred from Jack White's like everyone else?' – and the entire pub erupted with laughter.

If she hadn't barred you, she would stick the boot in in other ways. Andrew Manson recalls being in a drinking round with a group of five others. Every time they went up and ordered the same round of drinks, the price went up. Someone asked Catherine why, and she said, 'If you don't like it, you can fuck off.' They left their drinks there and walked out. In the same way, the night the pub first opened, locals got their first pint free, and afterwards there was a 20p surcharge on the normal price of every drink.

Taxi drivers passing pubs in Wicklow make it their business to count the number of cars outside each to see where the potential custom is for later in the night. Even before Tom's murder, the most you'd see outside Jack White's on a Saturday night was five cars, as against over twenty outside Lil Doyle's. Catherine had barred them all. But one Sunday night in the summer of 1995, one of the taxi drivers noticed the car park was as full as in the old days. He asked what was going on and was told that it was a party for some big crook, Dutchy Holland, who was now living in Brittas Bay.

After Tom's murder, Andrew believed Catherine's attitude had genuinely softened and an effective amnesty on everyone previously barred came into effect. He stated: 'I came into the bar and the regulars were asking, "Aren't you barred?", worried she was going to start shouting. But she just asked me, "Well, what do you think I'll get?" She was talking about her pending trial for murder. I said, "Four years, Catherine. The issue is whether an upstanding member of the community like yourself will be believed over terrorists and criminals."'

As ever, when she was the centre of attention, whether negative or positive, Catherine rewarded Andrew with a big feed and non-stop free pints. According to Manson, she went on: 'She said, "Even if I say Tom was dying anyway?" and she gave an example called the Empire State theory. She said: "What if there was a man in the third floor of the Empire State building pointing a new shotgun out a third-floor window? What if somebody who had decided to commit suicide jumped from the roof of the building? What if, as they sailed past the third-floor window, the man with his gun decided to test its shot and aim at the body flying by? The coroner would say the man had died of a gunshot, but the truth was the man was going to die anyway because he had jumped."

'I said, "How does this apply to you, Catherine?" And she said, "What if I say Tom had learned he was terminally ill but didn't want to die in agony, so he put a hit on his own life so I could collect on the insurance?" She said, "You can't kill someone already dying." I said, "Catherine, you'd be better off saying that you're mad and that you shot him yourself. That way you'd be out after eighteen months."

'Can you believe it, she was already working out the possible schemes she could come up with? I couldn't believe it; it was like an admission of murder from where I was sitting.

'She went on to talk about all the B&B guests who had ever stayed in Jack White's, over a thousand, to give an idea of how many keys to the place had gone missing. I told her she'd need receipts.'

Catherine's personality had made her notorious in Brittas Bay by the end of her ten-year reign. The week before the murder, she rang Ballyrogan House to enquire about an aerobics class. It was the Thursday before the bank holiday weekend. The fifteen professional women in regular attendance were informed that Catherine Nevin would be joining them next week; not one of them turned up for the class.

Even people she didn't know had cause to dislike her. A driver passing by stopped by the pub to use the phone. It was the late 1980s, long before the mobile phone craze. He needed to use the phone because a tragedy had occurred at home. He stopped at the pub and asked Catherine for change. She said she had none. He explained to her the urgency of his predicament, but she still refused to give him change for the phone. He asked to be served a drink, so he could buy change. Catherine said she wasn't serving drink, although there were customers drinking all around him. He ordered a meal. She said she wasn't serving food, although there were people eating around him. He moved on to the next pub and phoned from there. Some months later when the man was visiting friends in Wicklow, they teased him for not being able to get Catherine Nevin to give him change for a phone call, despite his reputation as a ladies' man. So he had a bet with them that he could have her if he wanted. He went to the bar and gave her the eye. Within minutes she was eating out of his hand.

'It was disgusting; he was half her age. She was pawing him across the bar and leaning over to let her boobs hang out. She was a disgrace,' says Attracta Manson.

After the murder, a 40ft by 20ft poster happened to be put up outside the pub with the slogan 'Killer on the loose', in an attempt to encourage speeding drivers to slow down! Catherine had it removed on the same day. A month later a Fianna Fáil election campaign poster went up, proclaiming, 'Crack Down on Crime' – and it met with the same fate! Many of the locals enjoyed the coincidence.

4

THE EQUALISER

Members of the gardaí are not allowed to join a union. Instead, a Garda Representative Association (GRA) member is assigned to investigate whether a guard is being victimised and is entitled to the backing of the association. In the Murphy and Whelan case, Detective Garda Jim McCawl, an Offaly man based in Arklow, was despatched. His efforts would earn him the nickname 'The Equaliser'. McCawl had twenty-five years' service under his belt when Catherine Nevin first started making allegations about members of the force. Coincidentally, Inspector Tom Kennedy had been McCawl's first sergeant. McCawl had been a plainclothes detective since 1975, and he had a wide range of experience. He had done stints on the border and had worked on the team that brought two Englishmen, John Shaw and Geoffrey Evans, to justice for the murder of Elizabeth Plunkett in Brittas Bay in 1976. But it was his capacity for endurance – he has raised over £100,000 in charity cycles for Our Lady's Hospital for Sick Children in Crumlin – that would turn him into a permanent thorn in the side of Catherine Nevin. Once he discovered she was a fraud, he would bide his time and wait until the moment was right to act.

After investigating the claims of innocence by Gardas Mick

Murphy and Vincent Whelan, McCawl became convinced that not only was Catherine Nevin rambling, but that she was delusional. His investigations into her attempts to cover up the fact that her husband had punched barman Larry D'Arcy led to a perjury case against her. The case is documented in Chapter 6.

But McCawl was also behind another startling discovery in relation to Catherine's claim that Garda Mick Murphy had sexually assaulted a girl in the back of a squad car in 1989. McCawl discovered that Patrick Doyle, of Redcross, Wicklow – a fisherman who lost an arm in a boating accident – had a different story to tell. The fisherman related a conversation he alleges he and his wife, Caroline, had with the girl on 22 August 1992.

In his statement, Doyle said:

'On 22nd August, 1992 my wife and I went to Jack White's for a drink. It was Saturday night and we were there for a while when we met the barmaid, whom we know for some time. We were talking for a while and she told us she was going to Wicklow. I told her it was raining but nevertheless she left. She returned after a while as she said she could not get a lift. She was talking to my wife and myself and we had a drink together and she then asked us if we were going to the Arklow Bay later on and we said we might. She asked us for a lift and we said okay. At approximately 11.30 we went to the Arklow Bay Hotel and we stayed there until the dance was over. There were a lot of cars and people knocking around and I made the remark: it's a wonder there are no guards around. [The girl] then made a remark not to mention guards as I have seen enough of them all week. I asked her where she saw them and she asked us did we not hear the crack about Mick Murphy and Catherine (ie, Catherine Nevin of Jack White's). My wife and I said you hear several stories but you never hear the truth. On 22nd August, 1992 … [the girl] said that if she told us the truth would we promise not to tell anyone because if Catherine found out she would kill her. We (Doyle and his wife) were out on the main road at this stage and we pulled over to the hard shoulder. Before [the girl] started to tell us the story she asked us again to promise not to tell anyone and especially not Catherine, and we agreed. She said Catherine got Murphy suspended for three months over money he wanted and the fact that Murphy wanted oral sex with [her]. I said what do you mean, money from Catherine? She said she wasn't sure as Catherine did not explain everything to her but she thought Catherine was supposed to have paid money to Murphy for doing something for her but he wanted more money and she wouldn't pay him and she reported him. I said what about you and Murphy and I asked her when had she and Murphy had sex. She said, "Do you think I am mad or what? I never had anything to do with Murphy." I said, "But I thought you told us you had." She said, "No, it is not like that. Catherine told the guards from Dublin that Murphy forced me to have oral sex with him about two and a half to three years ago and I had to make a statement about it because I could not let Catherine down." I said to [the girl], "What about when it goes to court, you could be in serious trouble, especially if they find out the truth." She said it would not be going to court because it is private and it is only between Catherine and myself [the girl] and Murphy and will only have to go to a private meeting. I told [her] "If that goes wrong you could be in very serious trouble because it might go to court and then it will be all over the papers." [The girl] said she could not let Catherine down as Catherine was always good to her and Catherine had put her up to saying these things. I told [the girl] that if they found out the truth that she would never get a job and her name would be ruined for life. [The girl] said that Catherine promised her that if she stood by her she would pay for her to go back to college for two years or if she wanted she could have a full-time job in the bar in Jack White's. I told [the girl] to be very careful of what she was letting herself in for and she said she would and we again promised not to tell anybody. On 5th September 1992 my wife and I went to Jack White's for a drink and as there was no one there we left and went to the Tap public house. We were there for a while when [the same girl] came over to us and I asked her was she having a drink and who she was with. She told us that she was with Catherine Nevin and she agreed to have a drink and one for Catherine. She stayed at the counter talking to my wife and I sat talking to Catherine. Catherine Nevin was intoxicated at the time and she told me that she had been up in Dublin giving statements about the other bastard. I asked her who and she said Murphy. She said, "For what he has done to [the girl] he will never wear a uniform again." She stated that if only the locals knew the sums of money she had to pay him for not summonsing locals who were leaving Jack White's with beer in them. Catherine Nevin said she knew about ten different Protestants that he tried to get money from for different things. She stated the sooner the better he was fucked out of the guards, that the barracks and Jack White's would be better places for it. She stated that Murphy would go down for life for what he did to [the girl]. I said to Catherine Nevin that [the girl] told us that that was nearly three years ago and if that was the truth why wait until now. She stated that there was a time and a place to do the bastard. I went back up to my friends at the bar, and my wife and [the girl] sat down with Catherine. Some time later my wife came to me very upset and stated that [the girl] and Catherine had accused us of making phone calls to [the girl]'s mother. I asked [the girl] what did she mean by this. [She] was crying and was drunk at this time. She told me that Catherine and herself thought that I rang her mother about what was going on in Jack White's. I told [the girl] that I didn't know her surname nor did I know her mother nor did I know her mother's phone number. Catherine Nevin came up to us then and she accused me of ringing [the girl]'s aunt. I said the same about her aunt as I didn't know her surname either. We decided to leave the Tap and go back to Jack White's. Inspector Tom Kennedy, who came into the premises shortly before, asked us to bring [the girl] back up to Jack White's, but we refused in view of what had happened. We went back to Jack White's but left after a short while. The following day, 6th September 1992, Tom Nevin and [the girl] came up to our house. [The girl] said she came to apologise and to explain about the phone call. They said they were not really sure who made the call but that it was made in Arklow. I said we didn't want to know anything about a phone call or anything else. I pointed out to her that she told us a fortnight ago about what had happened between Murphy and Catherine and herself and that she asked us not to tell anyone. I asked Tom Nevin what he thought about the whole matter and he said he was sick of the whole matter but there was nothing he could do about it. I asked [the girl] in front of Tom Nevin and my wife did anything happen between herself and Murphy. She said no but she had to back Catherine. I informed them that we would not be accused of anything and if there was any more trouble that I would take the matter further. The next day, the 7th September, myself and my wife were pulling into Jack White's carpark at lunch time when Inspector Tom Kennedy came over to us. He said, "The very man I want to see, Paddy, you were doing a lot of talking over the weekend ..." I said you have got it wrong, it was Catherine and [the girl] who were talking not me. He said, "Now I know all about it, I've been told." I said you have been told wrong ...'

In May 1994, almost two years after the inquiry into Murphy and Whelan first started, during which time they had been demoted to desk duties, the Director of Public Prosecution's office decided it would not prosecute the men on the basis of Catherine Nevin's claims. The reasons could not have been more stark: 'Proceedings should not be taken against either of these men. The witnesses are lacking in credibility and reliability' – a clear reference to the official recognition that Catherine Nevin had perjured herself in the pub brawl case taken by Larry D'Arcy against Tom Nevin.

But if Murphy and Whelan thought they had now been vindicated, they were to learn just how much they had under-estimated Catherine Nevin. She was at her most dangerous when she was losing. And nobody knew where the next strike would come from.

The blow, when it came, happened sooner than anyone expected. Within weeks of the Director of Public Prosecution's ruling, Murphy and Whelan were told that they were to be transferred to Enniscorthy and Carlow. Although, on the one hand, their suspensions from normal duties had been lifted, the transfers implied that their authorities still believed them cul-pable. If the men accepted the transfers, the implication was an admission of guilt and a virtual end to any prospects of promo-tion. They challenged their authorities in the High Court. As affidavits flew between the two sides, Whelan and Murphy learned that they were being moved because of allegations that apparently had nothing to do with Catherine Nevin. A com-plaint had been made from another member of the community, who stated that their continued presence was a serious source of disquiet in the local community. The complainant was one Mary Duffy from Redcross. But nobody had ever heard of her.

5

THE MYSTERY LETTER

Had a conversation between a pensioner and a postmistress in the little village of Redcross, just five miles from Jack White's, never occurred, detectives might never have untangled one of Catherine's most elaborate webs of deceit. But the conversation revealed just how bad a loser the Black Widow was.

It all started when Gardas Mick Murphy and Vincent Whelan learned that they were about to be transferred. On the one hand, they had been vindicated as no prosecution was to be made; on the other hand, they felt they were being punished. But the guards were told that the move had nothing to do with Catherine Nevin. Instead, they learned, a second local person had made a serious complaint about them in the form of a letter. The appearance of the mystery letter coincided with the Director of Public Prosecution's decision, in May 1994, not to take a case against the two guards and came as a bad blow to the two men who thought their days as the Walking Dead were finally nearing an end.

But whenever Catherine Nevin was involved, even on the periphery, Detective Garda Jim McCawl and his colleagues knew better than to take anything at face value. They started to investigate. They discovered that the letter purported to be from one Mary Duffy of Ballycapple, Barndarrig, in Redcross,

County Wicklow. Redcross is a small village, and everyone knows everyone else. But nobody knew who Mary Duffy was.

The guards called to the postmistress in Redcross, Mary Breen, wife of the local undertaker, Billy Breen. The postmistress informed detectives that their hunch was correct. There was no Mary Duffy of Ballycapple, Barndarrig, in Redcross. Amazingly though, the postmistress had heard the name Mary Duffy before. Ellen Duffy, a local pensioner in her seventies, of Ballycapple, Barndarrig, in Redcross, had received a letter addressing her as Mary Duffy and she had sought the postmistress's assistance. The postmistress, like the pensioner, was none the wiser having read the letter. It came from Garda headquarters in Phoenix Park, and informed one Mary Duffy that her complaint against two members of the gardaí, Vincent Whelan and Mick Murphy, was receiving their priority attention. But Ellen Duffy, who is since deceased, had never written to the gardaí to complain about Mick Murphy and Vincent Whelan. Somebody had used her name, with an incorrect first name, and her address.

The postmistress told McCawl that she had sent the letter back to Garda headquarters stating as much, and she said that two guards had been sent down from Dublin to investigate the case of the pensioner, the postmistress and the mystery letter. Both Mary Breen and Ellen Duffy explained the situation to the gardaí: that Ellen Duffy had not written the letter and that no Mary Duffy lived in Redcross.

Had the likes of Jim McCawl not known from experience that Catherine Nevin's entire life was spun on the single principle of deceit, the letter might never have been exposed. The case attempting to force the men's transfer fell apart. The transfers could not proceed and the two guards were returned to full duties. In the space of sixteen months, they had been cleared both by the Director of Public Prosecutions and the High Court. The fisherman, Patrick Doyle, had made a statement that contradicted the allegations concerning the girl who had alleged sexual assault. It seemed that the epic had exhausted all story lines. But the repercussions of the final twist continued to unfold.

Murphy and Whelan were soon back on the beat and returned to full duties. Following the lifting of their suspension, they brought their first batch of traffic cases before Judge Donnchadh Ó Buachalla at Arklow court. At this sitting, the judge made them swear the oath for every single case rather than just once, as in the case of their colleagues. They later complained about this as they felt it belittled them. On 3 November 1995, Ó Buachalla dismissed twenty-two of the twenty-six cases they brought before him. Six cases were brought by Garda Vincent Whelan, and twenty by Garda Michael Murphy for breaches of the Road Traffic Act, one of which related to driving without insurance or licence, and was adjourned for six months when the defendant failed to make an appearance.

Murphy and Whelan each made an official complaint to Garda headquarters that they felt they had been unfairly treated by the judge. Subsequently, Murphy and Whelan were informed that they were again to be suspended from normal duties and confined to the desk. They were also informed that they were to be transferred to Enniscorthy and Carlow, which the men opposed. The two gardaí sought a judicial review in the High Court with a view to being returned to full garda duties.

According to the Garda Representative Association, the men were also considering suing the State. They had not then received a copy of the original letter signed by 'Mary Duffy'. Nor had they received a copy of the postmistress's explanation to garda authorities. They had not got copies of the statements made by the pensioner and postmistress to the two investigating gardaí, nor the names of those gardaí who travelled down from Dublin to interview the women. The typeface of Mary Duffy's letter was being examined by garda experts.

An assault case brought by Garda Mick Murphy, which was due to be heard before Judge Ó Buachalla in Arklow District Court on 4 May 2000, was transferred to another court after pressure was put on the Department of Justice, according to the Garda Representative Association.

Those gardaí who felt they could not get justice from the criminal system felt they had to seek justice elsewhere: Detective Garda Jim McCawl decided to sue Catherine Nevin for defaming him; Gardas Michael Murphy and Vincent Whelan decided to sue the State for the treatment they received.

Even at the end, when on trial for her husband's murder, Catherine Nevin refused to lie down under the truth. A central plank in her defence was that the Arklow gardaí had a grudge against her and had conspired to 'stitch her up'. She claimed she had refused to give a statement to Arklow gardaí because she feared that it would be 'doctored'. Many gardaí believe that Catherine deliberately cast herself in the role of champion against corruption in the force so that should she ever be charged with the murder she was planning, she could claim she had been set up.

On 4 July 2000, eight years after being first instructed to work behind the desk, Gardas Mick Murphy and Vincent Whelan were reinstated to full policing duties. The timing of their exoneration was significant: they were returned to normal duties the day before the first sitting of a judicial inquiry set up to examine the circumstances surrounding the decision by Arklow Judge Donnchadh Ó Buachalla to put the Jack White's pub license into Catherine Nevin's sole name after she had been charged with the murder of her husband, and to examine the complaints of Gardas Whelan and Murphy.

'We feel completely vindicated and are looking forward to doing the job we took an oath to do,' Garda Murphy said publicly. Garda Vincent Whelan's wife, Michelle, was less magnanimous. 'Nobody knows what my family has suffered. I have watched Vincent age as his hair went grey and then white. We went through some tough times, especially with two small children and a mortgage.' On learning that the restrictions had been lifted, Michelle said she went from laughing to crying and then back to laughing again. 'I couldn't believe it was all over, that we had been given back our lives.'

Following the men's reinstatement, the strangest twist of the entire saga took place on 3 October 2000. That was the morning the second module of the inquiry was due to get under way. Its function was to hear the specific complaints of unfair treatment which the two gardaí had made against the judge – but the men's barrister announced that they were now withdrawing all allegations and that they did not want a 'stain or blemish' to attach to Judge Ó Buachalla's actions. Eoin McGonigal SC, barrister for Murphy and Whelan, had been presented just days earlier with a report drawn up by Chief Superintendent Martin Crotty, head of the Garda Internal Investigations Division in 1994, effectively being put on notice of Ó Buachalla's intention of introducing details of allegations then made against them. On the advice of their barrister, the men decided to let sleeping dogs lie and to concentrate their efforts instead on their civil case against the State. Justice Frank Murphy stated that he would have to consider whether the second module could be dropped in such a manner, but on 23 October, the final date of the hearing, he announced simply that the report on the inquiry would be complete in a matter of weeks. That same evening, Judge Ó Buachalla celebrated by cracking open a bottle of champagne with his senior counsel, John Rogers.

In December 2000 Supreme Court Justice, Mr Justice Frank Murphy, who chaired the public inquiry, published his findings on the pub license transfer controversy. He concluded that, although Judge Ó Buachalla had made errors of judgement, no injustice was done. In light of his friendship with Catherine Nevin, Ó Buachalla should not have heard the licensing application on her behalf, Justice Murphy reported. But it was 'an error of judgement and not an act of misconduct'. Mr Justice Murphy also said that the hearing of the application in camera in September 1997 was not justified and had damaged the judge's reputation. 'It is an oversight which he has every reason to regret,' Justice Murphy stated. He also recommended that Judge Ó Buachalla be awarded all his costs from the public inquiry but stated that, in his view, the Minister for Justice was 'not responsible for any other costs incurred by the gardaí.'

Then, just as it seemed that a line had been drawn under the entire sorry saga, an incident occurred on 26 November 2000 in the Beehive pub, just five miles from Jack White's, which cast another shadow over one of the gardaí concerned. It was just over a month since Gardas Murphy and Whelan had backed out of their hard-won public inquiry at the eleventh hour, and weeks away from publication of the inquiry's findings. Out of the blue, on 26 November, Garda Mick Murphy verbally threatened members of staff and assaulted the landlady. Witnesses claim he took offence at a seemingly innocuous comment. He was later convicted under the Public Order Act and again suspended from duty. Like all of the tall tales spun by Catherine Nevin, again it seemed she had based her fiction on a grain of truth.

But more twists in the plot were yet to come. When the owners of the Beehive attempted to have an aspect of their pub license renewed, they discovered their application had been opposed by a Wicklow man named Mick Murphy. He turned out to be not the ill-fated garda, but his father. In any event, the license was renewed.

6

PLOTS AND SCHEMES

In the pub trade, being able to subdue a brawl is part of the job description. But on one occasion, Jack White's landlady actually pitted her normally mild-mannered husband against one of his own barmen, Larry D'Arcy. The squabble concluded in a court of law after the barman sued Tom Nevin for hitting him. Catherine offered a bribe for a different version of events from car mechanic Anthony Doyle, who she claimed had witnessed the fight, although he later admitted he was nowhere near the pub. Doyle changed his story and confessed everything to gardaí after Catherine refused to pay him the full amount of the bribe offered. The outstanding debt was £230. It was a paltry sum to her, but her refusal to pay it marked the beginning of her downfall.

The whole thing started when Catherine began to shout at barman Larry D'Arcy on 23 December 1988. Tom and Catherine had just returned from a funeral in Kildare. D'Arcy had been left in charge of the pub. Catherine got it into her head that D'Arcy had been talking about private business to the customers and she started to berate him. Her outburst was controlled in that she made sure it occurred within her husband's earshot and it was calculated to hit Tom Nevin's Achilles' Heel – fear of gossip. Tom couldn't bear people knowing his private business; it was one of the reasons he had stayed with an unfaithful, domineering wife. The public humiliation of a second marriage break-up was something he was not willing to put his elderly mother through. On one occasion, according to Tom himself, he had barred a local from the pub for 'sticking his nose into other people's affairs without knowing the facts.' He would have to admit this when Larry D'Arcy took him to court for punching him.

It was lunchtime. Larry D'Arcy was sweeping the kitchen floor, doing his best to ignore Catherine's taunts about gossiping. Suddenly, Tom came rushing out of the spirits store and roared, 'When are you going to stop mouthing?' He pinned Larry against the cold-room door despite Larry's protestations that he had not said anything and didn't know what Tom was talking about. Tom hit him anyway, with his fist, on the face, head and chest, and on the left-hand side of his body. When Larry fell to the ground, Tom kicked him in the back and the legs. Catherine grabbed her husband by the arm and told him to 'Leave him alone, he's not worth it.' Such public displays of empathy for her husband were only as rare as Tom lashing out. Catherine had evoked the desired but unanticipated reaction from her husband, and this was his reward.

But Larry D'Arcy was not so easily consoled. Knowing how friendly Catherine was with the local gardaí, he decided to pursue the matter as a civil rather than criminal case. He refused to make a statement to gardaí – instead he sued Tom.

Tom Nevin was genuinely sorry for what he had done, but told customers that if he had 'hit Larry a few digs', the £2,500 damages being sought was a very high price to pay. Still, he was willing to fork out to put an end to the lawsuit then and there, but his wife would not be held to ransom and was already cooking up a plan to prevent Larry D'Arcy from getting a penny. She needed an alternative scenario that would explain away D'Arcy's obvious injuries. She was, by now, expert at knowing where to look for back-up when in a corner.

She approached Anthony Doyle, a local mechanic from the nearby village of Kilpatrick, who had been barred from Jack White's by Larry D'Arcy. Doyle had his own axe to grind with D'Arcy. But Catherine also chose Doyle because she knew that he himself was at the mercy of the law – when drunk, he had crashed a customer's car for which he was not insured. Doyle was supposed to service the car, instead he wrote it off. Everyone knew Jack White's was a 'garda pub'. Catherine made sure everyone also knew that she was owed a few favours. She told Doyle that if he helped her out in Tom's case, she'd pull whatever strings she could to get him out of his pending court appearance.

She offered Doyle £300 to perjure himself in the D'Arcy case, giving him £70 up-front and promising him the rest when the case was over. Anthony Doyle was glad of the money and of being allowed back into the nearest pub to his home. He later told gardaí, 'I know it was wrong. I was hard on the drink at the time.'

But Catherine had only just begun. Her mind was in its most natural state when spinning out the finer details of a mental drama and covering all eventualities. She took Anthony Doyle for a drive and relayed more of her plan to him. She said she had been thinking about the story. They couldn't pretend Doyle had fought with Larry inside the pub because he was barred at the time and it didn't add up. He would have to say he was passing Jack White's when he saw Larry hanging out clothes behind the pub. He would have to say it was dark, to explain why D'Arcy had mixed him up with Tom, and he would have to say that the towels on the line were white, to explain how he first saw D'Arcy's silhouette in the dark. He could say they had a row, Catherine added. He could say that Larry took a swipe at him first.

Doyle's statement to gardaí alleges: 'Catherine asked me

would I come to court because Larry had got me barred in the first place. She asked me would I say that I had assaulted her husband. She said there'd be a few old drinks in it for me if I gave evidence.'

On the day of the court case, Anthony Doyle arrived into Jack White's. The one-armed fisherman, Patrick Doyle, who had made a statement about the girl who had alleged assault by Garda Mick Murphy, was present. The fisherman asked Anthony Doyle what he was doing in the pub, saying he thought he was barred. 'I am the man who hit Larry D'Arcy,' Anthony Doyle replied. Catherine arrived into the bar and, seeing Doyle talking to the fisherman, asked: 'What do you think? This is my surprise.'

The civil case came before District Justice Sean Magee. Tom Nevin denied that he had punched, kicked, kneed or pushed Larry D'Arcy. Tom said that at 1.00am he had been counting the till for the day, which he normally did in the kitchen. He had asked Larry D'Arcy to empty the overflow can in the cold room, and, when he checked, he saw it was not done and the storeroom had flooded. He had a few words with D'Arcy, maybe shouted, but he had not threatened him, he said. He definitely had not hit him, he said. Catherine Nevin backed up Tom's version of events.

Then Anthony Doyle gave his evidence. Doyle said he was heading for the Tap pub when he saw Larry D'Arcy hanging out clothes. He said he called D'Arcy a name because he was annoyed that he was the cause of him being barred. He said that D'Arcy made a swipe at him first. The judge ruled in favour of Tom Nevin. But D'Arcy went for an appeal.

When the case came before the circuit court a year later, the star witness, Anthony Doyle, was less fluent under cross-examination. He crumbled under pressure, admitting that he had lied in parts. He denied that he was offered any induce-ment to give the evidence. Judge Patrick Smith said he did not believe Anthony Doyle. He said that Doyle had lied and had even admitted under cross-examination that he had lied. He said he was satisfied it was Tom Nevin who had hit Larry D'Arcy. He awarded D'Arcy his claim of £2,500 plus costs.

The entire matter might have ended there if Anthony Doyle had not asked Catherine to pay him the remaining £230 she had promised him. Catherine said there was no question of her paying the outstanding sum. 'We lose, you lose,' she told him, standing him a drink instead.

Welshing on the £230 owed would cost Catherine a lot more than she had bargained for. Anthony Doyle cooperated with the guards when they came calling five years after the assault on D'Arcy. It was 1993, almost two years after Tom Nevin lost the appeal, when Jim McCawl started looking into the D'Arcy case, which most people believed was well and truly over. The Nevins had lost; it seemed there was nowhere left to go. In the immediate aftermath the rumour mill had been rife about Anthony Doyle's part in it, but, as there was nothing concrete to back it up, no charges were ever brought against Catherine Nevin.

By 1993, Catherine had made seven statements alleging corruption against both Mick Murphy and Vincent Whelan and sexual assault against Murphy. One included a claim that she had paid the men £1,000 cash to 'look after' the D'Arcy case for her. Now everything that she had done which showed her to be unreliable became of paramount importance. The men's jobs were on the line. If Catherine could be shown to have perjured herself, her very credibility would be completely discredited.

McCawl was given the go-ahead to investigate the allegations of perjury. But his hands were effectively tied as perjury is one of the few crimes left without any power of arrest. Suspects cannot be detained against their will. However, when he approached Anthony Doyle, McCawl found him still bitter about the whole experience. Doyle admitted giving false evidence at Arklow District Court and Wicklow Circuit Court.

He said he was 'put up to' perjuring himself by Catherine Nevin and he made a statement to that effect.

A full-scale perjury investigation was now underway. This time the 'surprise' witness was Catherine, who would now have to be questioned. McCawl knew better than to take her on alone, given her history of inventing any version of events she pleased in order to cast herself in the role of victim, so he made sure he brought a witness. Inspector Ger Dillane accompanied him to Jack White's on 25 May 1993.

True to form, Catherine sent over some specials. 'The smell of whiskey would have knocked out a horse,' McCawl said. The rubber plant on the counter received an unexpected watering. 'You must have liked that,' Catherine said, sending him another. But she had picked the wrong man. McCawl is a teetotaller.

Catherine was informed by the guards that they were investigating allegations that she had perjured herself in the Larry D'Arcy case. She laughed. She said she was only her husband's witness and that her solicitor had the details. She asked for a piece of paper and a biro and wrote down the name and address of the solicitor. McCawl asked her why Anthony Doyle would lie about her.

She replied: 'I had no conversation with Anthony Doyle about my husband's case. Watch my lips. I had no conversation with Anthony Doyle or any other person only my solicitor and Tom about my husband's case.' The guards invited her to make a statement. She declined.

McCawl and Dillane then interviewed Tom Nevin. He greeted them with, 'What's the matter, lads?' They explained that they were investigating a perjury case and that there were allegations made against his wife, Catherine. Tom Nevin was told there were no allegations against him personally and he replied, 'I should hope not.' The guards asked him whether he was present when Anthony Doyle was offered money to perjure himself by Catherine. Tom's reply was firm: 'That refers to a previous case and it has been dealt with,' he said. 'The perjury case has not been dealt with,' McCawl told him. 'If that is the case, as far as I am concerned, this case has been dealt with and I was the loser in it. Good day, gentlemen,' Tom Nevin said.

Later, Catherine Nevin did make a statement. She stated: 'I am the joint proprietor with my husband of Jack White's Inn. We run a bar and restaurant business there. Anthony Doyle, Kilpatrick, Arklow, is a regular customer in the bar.' Despite the fact that she had called Doyle as a witness to defend Tom Nevin in the Larry D'Arcy case, she went on to say: 'He is a chronic alcoholic and is often under the influence when he appears in the forenoon. I am aware from his conversation that he drinks a lot of poiteen in his home. He stated yesterday 8/9/93 that he had been drinking poiteen at home for the past ten days. He once worked as a motor mechanic and still repairs cars at his home.'

She went on: 'In December 1972, Anthony Doyle had an old Renault car ... for repairs. He crashed the car at Mervyn Sutherland's gateway at Ballinavalley on his way home from a pub in Redcross village. It was badly damaged and I understand that he was not covered by insurance.'

Anthony Doyle phoned Catherine Nevin to let her know that he was cooperating with the investigation. 'She said to me it would be all right and not to worry,' he said. But Inspector Tom Kennedy paid him a visit, he claims. Kennedy called to Doyle's car repair business, Doyle alleges, and he claims that Kennedy asked for an estimate to paint over the letters 'IRA' scratched on his car. But Kennedy says he did not ask for an estimate, although he admits he did speak to Doyle about his car. Doyle told gardaí: 'He (Kennedy) asked me to look at the scratch on the boot lid of his car which had been scratched with a nail. I looked at the boot lid. I told him I would do it the following Saturday.' Doyle added that the inspector also asked him what he had said in his statement.

The inspector, Doyle alleges, warned him to be very careful about what statement he signed. The inspector denied that any of this took place.

Catherine's next allegation proved that Detective Garda McCawl's first instincts that Catherine would turn on him because he was investigating her for perjury could have not been more accurate. Just as she had alleged Gardas Mick Murphy and Vincent Whelan were corrupt, now McCawl got some of the same treatment.

When Catherine made a statement for the perjury investigation on 20 March 1993, McCawl was her main target. She said that Anthony Doyle, the man who had exposed the bribe, had since told her another scenario. She falsely alleged that Doyle had claimed that Detective Garda Jim McCawl had threatened to charge him with drunk driving and driving without insurance if he did not cooperate with the investigation into the perjury charges. Catherine also claimed that Doyle had said he had signed a statement without knowing what was in it.

Catherine's attempt to discredit McCawl in her statement didn't finish there. She went on to say how Anthony Doyle also told her he had been 'taken out of bed by Garda Jim McCawl about nine or ten days previously at 8.30am. He said that McCawl told him that he was being taken to the station in connection with perjury in the Larry D'Arcy case.' She went on to say that Anthony Doyle told her how he had been handed £100 to cooperate with McCawl.

Nothing of the kind actually happened, and Detective Garda Jim McCawl took these false allegations so seriously that he decided to sue Catherine Nevin for damages – not for the money, but to protect his good name.

Inspector Tom Kennedy also made a statement to the gardaí which is quite similar to Catherine's. The inspector said details of the statements in the perjury investigation were read to him on 10 August 1993. In relation to the statements which the inspector described as 'purported' to have been by Anthony Doyle, Kilpatrick, Redcross, Co. Wicklow, he replied: 'The first statement dated 15/3/93 refers to some advice I was supposed to have given Anthony Doyle in connection with giving evidence in court in a civil case involving one Larry D'Arcy. I never discussed any matter concerning evidence with Anthony Doyle. I never knew Larry D'Arcy and I know little about the case. This would be a civil matter having nothing whatsoever to do with me. In a second statement dated 25 May 1993, reference is made to a conversation which I am alleged to have had with Anthony Doyle at his home. This conversation never took place. I would never use the expressions attributed to me. I am shocked and amazed to hear my name being used in this fashion. My car was slightly damaged about eighteen months ago by having the letters 'IRA' scraped with a nail or sharp instrument on the boot lid. Anthony Doyle saw the damage at that time and asked to be given the job of repairing it. I did not ask him to quote a price or make any arrangements with him. I never got it repaired. I did not want to give those responsible that I was worried or concerned about it.'

The inspector gave a reason why Anthony Doyle might have made such allegations: 'I first met Anthony Doyle at Arklow District court on 16 January 1989. He was a defendant on a charge of larceny (in Jack White's) which I prosecuted. He was convicted after a lengthy hearing and a thorough cross-examination by me. I believe that I am not regarded as his favourite policeman since then ... About December, 1992, Anthony Doyle was given a car to repair ... Anthony Doyle drove [this] car to a local licensed premises and crashed it into a wall on the way home and damaged it beyond repair. It appears that he was not covered by insurance to drive the car.'

Kennedy claimed Doyle had 'openly' discussed the way his statement was taken by McCawl in Jack White's. The inspector's story was similar to Catherine's.

◆　◆　◆

While the Nevins were in Jack White's, Catherine made fourteen insurance claims, only one of which was related to a robbery that had been reported to gardaí. Six claims were for damage caused by storms, flooding and a fire. Twelve times she managed to collect. In December 1993, Catherine lodged a claim against FBD Insurance for the robbery of jewellery, including her wedding ring, from the premises sometime between 4 December and 5 December. Catherine was subsequently seen wearing the wedding ring; on 31 June 1996 she told gardaí that Tom Nevin had recovered it for her after trawling through Dublin pawnshops and negotiating with his criminal contacts. 'He gave me a ring, it was identical to my stolen wedding ring,' she stated to gardaí. 'I asked him if he had got another one made. He said "No, that is the one I gave you twenty years ago." He just said, "There it is, wear it, now, I said I would get it back for you."'

There were thirteen other insurance claims:

DATE	CAUSE	SETTLEMENT
6 May 1986	theft	£1,200
11 February 1990	storm	£830
10 May 1990	–	–
11 February 1990	fire	£516
5 January 1991	storm	£1,090
1 December 1990	–	–
15 June 1991	theft	£1,647
4 October 1991	storm	£57.50
20 November 1991	cash	£1,500
15 June 1991	theft	£220
15 June 1991	theft	£124

DATE	CAUSE	SETTLEMENT
26 December 1992	–	£247.72
1 March 1993	flood	£350
–	–	£2,000

Robberies reported to the gardaí:

1986 – cigarettes, drinks, microwave, radio. Valued at £2,427.22. Nobody charged.

20 September 1987 – £100 from unlocked safe. Nobody charged.

23 September 1987 – two silver rings and £100 cash. Value £500. Nobody charged.

17 December 1988 – cash from behind counter. Two charged and convicted in Arklow District Court on 17 January 1989: Anthony Doyle and Michael Fortune.

30 June 1990 – stolen cheque presented, value £50. Nobody charged.

22 July 1990 – stolen cheque presented, value £50. Nobody charged.

15 June 1991 – larceny of cash register, 3 bottles of spirits and £50. Nobody charged.

23 March 1992 – larceny of parasol outside pub, value £80. John O'Neill convicted.

28 August 1992 – dud £20 note presented.

29 November 1994 – 4 crates of beer stolen, value £168.

14 April 1995 – burglary of house. Cigarettes (£22), cash (£40), wine (£15) two brass ornaments (£150), leather jacket (£150), provisional driving licence (£12) taken.

14 January 1995 – beer stolen from stores. Value £150.

Reconstruction

THE ACCOUNTING

Catherine had been refusing to sign the pub's accounts since the end of 1995. If Revenue landed on Jack White's doorstep, there would be trouble. Catherine didn't care. Revenue had already carried out an audit, but only because of Tom's mistake in the PAYE/PRSI figures in the first place. Now she said that somebody had informed the taxman to take a closer look.

When they bought the pub it was a low-keg spirits house with a local trade in Hicksville. She was the cosmopolitan one who saw the potential in the market for food, not drink. Singlehandedly, she felt, she had turned the pub into the local golf club's 'nineteenth hole' with her preparation of pub grub. She started using a technique taught on a course by Darina Allen, which involves preparing the food in a way that retains its natural juices. As well as that, it was Catherine's house on South Circular Road that had been sold to finance the £80,000 refurbishment of the kitchen. She, too, was the one who found out about the European grant they could apply for because of the truckers travelling to and from Europe via Rosslare.

In ten years, Jack White's had gone from £270,000 in value to over £600,000 and, as far as Catherine was concerned, it was all due to her. What was the point in complicating matters by starting a new year with two names on the accounts when it would end with only one? Paperwork had always been her weak point, whether it came to applying for an early-house exemption, restaurant licence or bar extension. Tom was good at that kind of thing, except when it came to drawing up a will. The most she could get him to do was take out a life insurance policy in 1995, even if it was only a cheap £70,000 one.

Catherine arranged a meeting with financial consultant Pat Russell in the Davenport Hotel in Dublin in early January 1996 to explain her predicament. She said Tom was 'drinking excessively' and wasn't pulling his weight in the business. She said that she 'would love to buy Tom out, but he wouldn't sell'. The money wasn't a problem, she told Russell. But the money was a big problem. As Catherine saw it, it was right-fully hers.

Russell had been the Public Relations Officer for the Sinn Féin cumann in Church Street, which he joined in 1983. He knew the Nevins through The Barry House. Catherine met him through John Jones in the Sinn Féin advice centre. Russell is a very clever man. He has a BSc in Management Science and a MA from Trinity College, Dublin; an NIHE-certified diploma in account management; a diploma in legal studies from the King's Inns; and is a graduate of the Marketing Institute of Ireland.

His business was equally varied. He had done a lot of tax settlement; at the first tax amnesty he was employed as a specialist, and had a property consultancy business in Merrion Square – matching buyers with financial packages – and he even had clients from as far away as the Ukraine.

In 1991 and 1992 he would drop into Jack White's for a meal on his way to a pub he had bought in Waterford. Catherine would never let him pay for his meals. Now, for her, it was payback time. She asked him, in the light of the ongoing problems, if he would consider taking over the pub's accounts.

Russell declined, but he said he knew an accountant who was suitable – Noel Murphy in Cork. He added a proviso: the pub could not change accountants without the consent of Jack White's joint proprietor, Catherine's husband, Tom Nevin.

This presented Catherine with a snag. She explained that she didn't want to trouble Tom with the matter until such time as she had found a solution. As always, she embellished, impressing upon Russell the need for secrecy until the matter was resolved. A member of staff had reported her to the Revenue in the first place, she told him. Russell agreed to use the alias John Ferguson whenever he rang the pub and that he would leave no messages.

Between the start of January and mid-March 1996, 'John Ferguson' rang Jack White's quite a lot. Staff were instructed to get Catherine when he called, no matter where she was, and while speaking to him she would always whisper. Russell went along with her idiosyncracies.

Eventually everything was ready to change accountants, but Tom did not show up for the prearranged meeting. Catherine said he was unable to attend because he had been drinking all night. Two further meetings were arranged with the Cork accountant Noel Murphy, but Catherine failed to show for both.

Pat Russell and Noel Murphy organised the third meeting in Jack White's so that there could be no excuse. On 14 March 1996, Murphy arrived into Jack White's to work out the Nevins' new game plan with both proprietors, but again, there was no Catherine. She had gone to visit Alan McGraynor, the barman, who was in Loughlinstown Hospital after a motorbike accident.

They agreed to reconvene at a later date. But, within a week, events would take on a life of their own and Catherine no longer needed to get the consent of the joint proprietor for any decision she would make. By this time, Tom Nevin was dead.

THE INSPECTOR AND
THE JUDGE

7

INSPECTOR TOM KENNEDY

At the height of the Tom Nevin murder investigation, a bitter row threatened to upstage the deliberations in the incident room. The battle concerned retired Inspector Tom Kennedy. The issue was whether or not he should be called in for questioning; the grounds – his association with Catherine Nevin. A head-count among the investigation team revealed a 16:5 split in favour of bringing him in. But the senior officers on the investigation team numbered the five against, and within the garda force such decisions are never democratic. Rank and experience always holds sway. Included in the five against were the incident-room handler, Detective Inspector Liam Hogan, and Detective Garda James (Bernie) Hanley, who has worked on the biggest criminal cases in recent years. Both are normally attached to the Investigation Unit in Garda headquarters. Also against was Detective Garda Tom Byrne, formerly of the murder squad and now retired. They were opposed to bringing him in because they feared a media blitz.

Up to this point in the trial, very little had been published in the media about the relationship between Tom Kennedy and Catherine Nevin because of the country's strict libel laws. But if Kennedy were brought in for questioning, the headlines would be sensational and the affair could easily be inferred. The garda chiefs could not see the long-term advantage of this. There was no suggestion that Tom Kennedy had done anything wrong, but the feeling on the ground was that he knew Catherine better than anyone and might have vital information in her regard. On the other hand, overexposure at this early stage could jeopardise the trial and give Catherine grounds to plead trial by media. The row subsided and Tom Kennedy was not brought in, but rank-and-file gardaí working on the case determined that no matter how deep they had to dig, they would keep digging. As it turned out, the investigators would barely have to scrape beneath the surface.

◆　◆　◆

Inspector Tom Kennedy served in Wicklow for over thirty years. As in other parts of the country during that time, Wicklow had its fair share of murders. In November 1985 a mother and daughter, Margaret and Ann Nolan, were murdered at their home in Ballymurrin, Kilbride. Just five years later, the Reverend Stephen Hilliard was stabbed in the neck during a break-in at his home in Rathdrum, where he had served for just two months. Catherine learned that even Jack White's had its own ghoulish past. Back in 1976 two Englishmen, John Shaw and Geoffrey Evans, slept in the car park of the pub after raping and murdering Elizabeth Plunkett, a Dublin girl on holidays in Brittas Bay. The killers drove on to the west and did the same to another girl, Mary Duffy, whose body they tried to anchor to the seabed with a lawnmower. (Strangely, this was the name used by the mysterious letter-writer in the Murphy–Whelan case. See chapter 5.)

In 1989 Inspector Tom Kennedy was the most senior guard in the Arklow area. He had responsibility for the Gorey district, taking into its ambit Arklow, Wicklow and Enniscorthy. His first posting as a garda had been to Wicklow; he was then promoted to sergeant in 1976 and posted to Letterkenny, County Donegal. He was then moved back to Wicklow, then

Enniscorthy, where members of the force serving under him remember him as a forward-thinking, fair-minded sergeant. He rose to the rank of inspector in 1989, a post he held for five years before retiring on age limit in March 1994. Former Chief Superintendent and retired head of the murder squad, John Courtney, a fellow Kerryman, remembers him as 'a good sound fellow with a great knowledge of the law.'

All his life, Tom Kennedy had done everything by the book. He had had a model career and educated two of his three children to be a solicitor and doctor. Then he met Catherine Nevin.

Although Kennedy claims he first got to know Catherine Nevin in 1991, he first met her in a professional capacity in 1988, when he spearheaded an investigation which necessitated him calling to Jack White's and interviewing the landlady in September of that year.

On 28 September, Catherine had reported to gardaí that a customer in the pub had been taken out at gunpoint. Her claims could not be corroborated and might have been dismissed as fantasy, had Catherine not dropped the name of a senior Provisional IRA paramilitary. It was like a bombshell. There seemed to be only one answer as to how a publican's wife in a holiday town could know the name of one of the Republican's most up-and-coming young stars, whose identity was presumed to be the preserve of the IRA and Special Branch – she had to be telling the truth.

The incident made the national press. Under the headline 'Kidnap Link To Guns Find', the Evening Herald of 29 September 1988 reported:

'A man taken at gunpoint from a pub on the Arklow–Dublin Road last night could be facing a paramilitary court martial, it is feared by Gardaí.

'The man was hustled out of Jack White's pub with a pistol to his head by a man who followed him into the premises. They were driven away by a third man in a blue car.

'Both men spoke with pronounced Northern accents and Gardaí are examining the possibility that the incident could be linked to the discovery of a bunker in Arklow during the recent nationwide search for arms, or less probably to INLA–IPLO rivalry.

'Roadblocks mounted last night failed to encounter the car, believed to be a Mercedes, and no matching missing person or stolen vehicle reports have been received.

'A Garda officer said it was likely Republicans in the Arklow area would be asked for assistance in the investigation today.'

Gardaí, however, were unable to find any substance to Catherine's story. The newspaper had been misled. Hindsight would show the remarkable similarities between this story and others which she spun at a later stage. In the preceding years the country's security had been at its most fragile – the racehorse Shergar, Don Tidey and Galen Weston had been kidnapped; the following year in England, ten people were killed when an IRA bomb ripped through the Royal Marine School of Kent. The fact that a publican's wife had come across information of this category had to be taken extremely seriously. Interviews with other customers in the bar did not back up her version of events, but Catherine Nevin did seem to know an awful lot about the IRA. A Special Branch file was set up under her name. She had already been mentioned in the file on Gerry Heapes, who had served time in the Provo wing in Portlaoise jail for his part in the armed robbery of Leyden's Cash and Carry. The person who had provided the information recorded in Catherine's file is not identified by name. 'You're talking about life-and-death stuff, there are never any names saying who's dealing with who, it's too dangerous,' a source explained.

After Tom Nevin's murder in March 1996, detectives went to look for a key Catherine Nevin file in the Crime and Security Section in 1997, but it could not be found.

Catherine's step-aunt, Patricia Flood, told gardaí she met Catherine and Tom Kennedy together around 1989 in a pub in Kildare, and the deepening of their friendship in 1989 is corroborated by Ciaran Barnes, a barman in Toss Byrne's, a pub situated on the Wexford side of the N11. In a statement to gardaí, he said that he got to know Catherine Nevin of Jack White's pub, as she was a regular caller. On several occasions she would call on her own and she would tell him she was waiting for Inspector Tom Kennedy. Tom Kennedy would call on his own sometimes, and Catherine Nevin would arrive to join him, and on numerous occasions they arrived together. He said that they would spend a lot of time in the pub when they came, and that they mostly had lunch, then would leave and come back, and usually spend up to four or five hours in the pub. They would always come into the lounge. Tom Kennedy would usually drink a pint of Smithwicks. Catherine would drink whiskey or wine, but could drink anything – she would vary her drink. Tom Kennedy did too, but not to the same extent. Barnes said that Tom Nevin would call on his own the odd time and have a sandwich, but that he never saw Tom Nevin there with Catherine or Tom Kennedy. He knew that Tom Kennedy used to drive a Renault car and Catherine Nevin drove an Omega. He said they would often arrive in separate cars, and when leaving they would kiss each other goodbye outside. He said he saw this happening on several occasions. They appeared to be very close to one another. Several times, he said, Kennedy and Catherine Nevin would come into the pub after lunch and stay until closing time.

In court, neither Kennedy nor Catherine denied their friendship or regular socialising. On the stand, Catherine could recall only a handful of occasions when they had met each other alone. Both denied any sexual affair.

But, coincidentally, Tom Nevin and Catherine Nevin

stopped sharing a bedroom in 1989, when Tom Kennedy and Catherine's friendship was in full flight. Cleaner Janey Murphy, who worked in Jack White's for the ten years of the Nevins' tenure, said in an interview: 'He [Kennedy] used to sneak down the stairs in the morning and out the front door and hang around outside for around ten minutes and then come back in, take his coat off and ask if Mrs Nevin was in.'

Although 1991 is the date Kennedy recalls as their first meeting, in fact by this date Catherine regarded him highly enough to register him as her protector and guardian on official forms. On 6 September 1991 she registered him as her 'next of kin' on admission to the Mater Hospital.

A former tenant of Tom Nevin's, Hugh Murphy, also had information about the relationship, although he was not called to give evidence. In a statement to gardaí, he said that he had moved into one of Tom's flats at Mountshannon Road in Rialto in 1990, after answering an ad in the paper. His flat was on the ground floor, second on the right inside the front door. Further down the hall, at the bottom of two flights of stairs, was the entrance to another flat. He told gardaí:

'This flat was always vacant and was used most weekends by Catherine Nevin and a man I know to be Tom Kennedy. At first I didn't know him but after some period of time I learned that he was in the Guards as I saw him on television in relation to some incident that happened in Wicklow.' He said that Kennedy used to come to the flat with Catherine Nevin in the car he recognised from television – Kennedy was interviewed on television and his car, a Renault, was in the background. Murphy remembered the registration, except for the first digit: 'BZS something-87' (he was unable to remember all the numbers). He said that sometimes the two would come in the Nevins' car with Catherine driving, and at other times in separate cars. They would arrive on a Friday evening around 6.00pm to 7.00pm and would stay for the weekend, usually leaving on a Monday morning or sometimes on a Sunday evening. He said that they stayed together in this flat for the weekend, staying overnight on a regular basis; that they'd go out in the evening and then he'd see them coming back after closing time and going into the flat. Murphy had an arrangement for putting out the bins for Tom Nevin, and after these weekends, on a Monday morning, he would find a lot of empty wine bottles and whiskey bottles, which was unusual in the house. Then he remembered once, while he was a tenant in Mountshannon Road, going to the Gate Bar on the Crumlin Road. The barman put a pint in front of him, and when he asked he was told it was from the couple behind him. Behind him were Catherine Nevin and Tom Kennedy, sitting close together, 'as close as you can get'. They smiled and acknowledged him, he said. On another occasion, he said, on one of Catherine's weekends at Mountshannon Road with Tom Kennedy, she came to his door looking for the rent, but he refused to pay her as his arrangement was to pay Tom Nevin on a Monday afternoon. Tom Nevin collected rent from 4.00pm onwards – any time within a few hours – maybe up to 6.00pm at the latest, when he'd be coming back from the Cash and Carry. He said that Catherine was aggressive and had a few drinks on her and that he closed the door on her face. He said he left the flat in Mountshannon Road in August 1992 to move to a bigger place with his girlfriend at the time, now his wife, and that Tom Nevin gave him the double bed from the flat to start them off in the new place. Tom, he said, was a very good landlord and very kind, and they parted on good terms.

Other former tenants of Tom Nevin's corroborated Hugh Murphy's claims. Linda Evans also rented a room at Mountshannon Road between February 1991 and April 1994. Hers was a two-room flat costing £28 per week, collected by Tom on Mondays, except on rare occasions when Catherine called. There were six flats altogether in the house. Evans told gardaí that there were five flats rented out and the sixth left vacant for Catherine. In her evidence in court she said: 'Catherine used to come up to the flat at least once a month, usually at the weekends. She'd usually stay over the Saturday night. More often than not she had a man with her. He stayed in the flat with her. I would describe this man as 6ft–6ft 2in, quite broad, slicked-back hair, going grey, in his mid-fifties. He sometimes wore glasses. He drove a silver car. He mostly wore a suit and he had a potbelly. I never actually spoke with this man, but I met him fairly regularly coming out of the flat. As far as I'm concerned Tom [Nevin] was a gentleman. Catherine on the other hand was a witchy kind of woman. She wasn't very nice.'

Aisling O'Connor also rented a flat from Tom between November 1992 to April 1995. Her rent was £30 a week, collected on Mondays by Tom Nevin. She made a statement, which is in the Book of Evidence. She was not called to give evidence, but she told gardaí:

'I got on very well with Tom. I didn't see eye to eye with his wife, Catherine. She wasn't in the flats – she was just there to collect the rent. The week I left the flat I had a party. One of the neighbours complained about the noise and Catherine Nevin rang me about 5.00am and said I was going to be evicted. Most weekends Catherine stayed over in a flat in the houses. She had another man with her. He used to drive a silver car. I would describe him the same as Linda [Linda Evans] did. I remember I met him one morning coming from the bathroom. He had a pair of boxer shorts on him and he had a peachy coloured dressing gown on him, which was way too small – I'd say it was Catherine's.'

In court, Tom Kennedy admitted that he was the man with the 'slicked-back hair' that Linda Evans described when she was called to give evidence, but he denied ever staying overnight. He had been to the flat in Mountshannon Road, he admitted, 'collecting rents', or when Catherine had problems with tenants, he said – 'she asked me to be there, this happened on two occasions at least.' He said he would call in the evening around 6.00pm or 7.00pm but that he never stayed the night. He would stay half an hour, up to three-quarters of an hour. He would wait in the hallway while she collected the rent and have a cup of coffee in the flat before he left; that was the sum of it, he said. He said he had had no sexual relations with Catherine. 'I am not into that kind of thing,' he said. 'I value my family and marriage. I have been married over thirty years, thirty-four years. I have three grown-up children, aged 30, 31, 33.'

Brendan Murphy, who owns the Horse and Hound Inn in Ballinaboola, about fifty miles from Jack White's, also had information about the pair. In court, Catherine claimed that the inn was a favourite retreat for herself and her husband. When asked if she had ever stayed on her own in the Horse and Hound at the same time as Inspector Kennedy, she said if she had, she could not remember. The owner of the inn told gardaí that back in the early 1990s he knew Tom Kennedy from Wicklow Garda station, and that when Kennedy was temporary acting Garda Superintendent for the New Ross Garda District he stayed at their premises on a number of occasions as a paying guest. He remembered that on one of those occasions he was joined by a woman who Murphy knew to be Catherine Nevin, the wife of Tom Nevin from Jack White's Inn, Arklow, County Wicklow – he knew Tom and Catherine Nevin from visiting Jack White's Inn on his trips to Dublin for business reasons. Murphy said that Catherine stayed with Inspector Kennedy for a period of two to three days, that they had separate rooms but were in one another's company. He said he didn't bother them and just got on with his business.

During her trial, Catherine Nevin was asked if she had ever stayed in the Horse and Hound under a different name. She said that she had never used a false name but if she had, her husband, Tom, must have invented the alias for her without her knowledge, and she could not explain why.

She was also quizzed about the Valley Hotel in Wooden-bridge, County Wicklow, and asked if she had ever been there with Inspector Tom Kennedy at a darts match. Again, she claimed that she could not recall. But Gerald Connolly, the barman who worked there for eleven years, told gardaí a different story. He said he recalled an incident in 1993 when the darts team from Jack White's were playing the Valley Hotel darts team. 'The match started about 9.30pm,' Connolly stated. 'Catherine Nevin was there in the company of Garda Inspector Tom Kennedy.' He said that after the match was over, about 11.30pm, Tom Kennedy and Catherine Nevin were in the lounge with the Jack White's team. They were all drinking, and Catherine bought a couple of rounds of drink for the team. He said that then Catherine Nevin started to 'play up to' one of the Jack White's team, and that after a while he could see Kennedy getting jealous at the carry-on of Catherine Nevin. At about 3.45am, he said, Tom Kennedy called him down and asked what time was closing time. Connolly laughed, but Kennedy repeated the question. When he knew Kennedy was serious, Connolly said 11.00pm. Kennedy pointed out that it was now much later – it was a quarter to four. He told Connolly to clear the place 'or I will get the law'. Connolly started to shout 'time', but the rest of the darts team said they were not going without Kennedy – they implied they were going to follow him so as not to get stopped by guards on the road if he was with them. In the end the team left, and then Tom Kennedy and Catherine Nevin left. Connolly said that they had their car parked right in front of the window of the lounge. He said he went in there to get the keys to lock the lounge door, he could hear Catherine shouting and screaming at Tom Kennedy. Everyone else had gone by now and they were the only people left. The argument continued outside. Both of them then drove off in the car. He did not know whether it was Catherine's car or Tom Kennedy's car.

They may have had their arguments, but Tom Kennedy

was Catherine's most strident defender when it came to protecting her. Two years earlier, on 4 October 1991, he had contacted Rita Halloran of the casualty ward at St James's Hospital in Dublin for exact details about Catherine's visit to the casualty ward. Halloran replied: 'Dear Inspector Kennedy, I saw Catherine Nevin in the Accident and Emergency department at St James's Hospital on the 31st August 1991. She complained of headache and neck pain. She stated that she had been assaulted by her husband on the previous evening and had sustained punches to back, arms and head. She had no memory of trauma to the neck. She also stated that she had been assaulted by her husband on a number of occasions in the past. Neurological examination was completely normal. X-Ray of cervical spine was reported as normal. She was prescribed Voltarol 50mg tds and advised to contact a social worker.' (This was the incident described in Chapter 3, when Garda Mick Murphy walked into Jack White's in the middle of the row, but declined to make a statement allegedly sought by Inspector Kennedy about the 'assault' on Catherine.)

Caroline Strahan, who worked in the pub between 1992 and 1994, said she believed Catherine Nevin had an affair with Kennedy. Strahan was fifteen years old when she went upstairs to Catherine's bedroom to tell her there was a phone call for her. In court she gave evidence, stating: 'From what I seen, Tom [Kennedy] didn't have any shirt on him and I can't remember about Catherine.'

The inspector denied that Caroline Strahan had seen him in bed without his shirt on. But he admitted to being in Catherine's bedroom as 'she frequently had bouts of illness and I visited her.' He said he always sat on a chair in her room beside her bed. (The photographs taken of her bedroom after the murder do not show a chair beside her bed.)

Eileen Byrne, who worked in Jack White's in 1994, said Inspector Kennedy was there most days when she arrived first thing in the morning.

By 1994 the effect on Tom Nevin was great. Catherine's step-aunt, Patricia Flood, told gardaí how Tom Nevin had put his face in his hands in despair when he confided in her the details of the affair. She claims that Tom Nevin said: 'How would you like to see Tom Kennedy coming out of Catherine's room in the morning?' Tom Nevin was crying, Flood said. This was Christmas 1994. Patricia Flood and Catherine's mother are half-sisters – they have the same father. But Flood was reared with Catherine, and the two are more like sisters than aunt and niece in age. Flood was shocked by what Tom Nevin was telling her. She knew the man he was talking about. Catherine had introduced her to Tom Kennedy, a man Catherine described as 'high up in the guards', around 1989. Catherine Nevin brought Kennedy to meet her step-aunt, Patricia Flood, in Morrison's pub in Suncroft, Kildare, where Patricia lives, just a few miles from where Catherine was brought up in Nurney. Flood understood Kennedy and Catherine to be just friends. But five years after that initial meeting, Catherine's husband was sitting on the couch in her kitchen crying, she told investigating gardaí. At one time, Tom Nevin and Catherine and Patricia Flood and her husband Mick, a mechanic, had all socialised together and gone to dances with each other, she explained. Tom Nevin and Mick Flood both shared a great interest in the GAA. After Mick died in 1989, Tom [Nevin] maintained the friendship with his wife's step-aunt. He continued to call every Christmas, although he was unaccompanied by Catherine. By Christmas 1994, the acrimony between Tom [Nevin] and Catherine had turned into something much more extreme – Tom Nevin seemed to Patricia Flood to be 'a broken man', she told gardaí. She added that Tom had confided in her that 'Catherine was wining and dining Tom Kennedy to the best and he had to put up with it. I said to him: "Is she trying to drive you mad?"' Flood was not called to give evidence.

Catherine revelled in the 'perks' of her new-found friendship. On the stand, she said the inspector would check out the backgrounds of people applying for jobs in Jack White's to see if they had criminal records. It emerged in court that Kennedy also provided escorts for the pub when they were making lodgements, and banked the money in the Garda safe in Wicklow at weekends; every superintendent's office is equipped with a safe.

But things did, apparently, cool down between Tom Kennedy and Catherine. Elizabeth Hudson, who worked in the pub from 1991, timed the cooling-off to the arrival of the new judge, Donnchadh Ó Buachalla, in the area. 'Tom Kennedy hasn't been visiting here as often since the judge came on the scene, but he has been coming back since the murder,' Hudson told gardaí. However practical the Jack White's connection was for the judge, it certainly looked as if Catherine was infatuated with him.

However, Inspector Kennedy was around when Detective Garda Joe Collins and Detective Sergeant Fergus O'Brien went to Jack White's on 4 December 1996 to put the allegations of Gerry Heapes and Willie McClean – the men she solicited to kill Tom – to Catherine. She was sitting at the bar with Tom Kennedy. The guards said they would like to speak to her in private. She said she was quite happy to speak in front of Tom Kennedy. They told her she didn't have to say anything. 'She alighted from the stool and went behind the bar and wrote down Garret Sheehan, her solicitor, on a piece of paper.' They asked her if that meant she didn't want to address the allegations. 'She said, "Yes, thank you very much. See my solicitor",' the guards reported.

In March 1994, Catherine organised Tom Kennedy's retirement party. His wife, Mary, was there, although they were fighting all night, according to a source. At the trial, Catherine Nevin claimed she was good friends with Mary Kennedy, but that she had never been invited into her house.

In fact, Mary Kennedy blamed Catherine for the split of her marriage. After the verdict, Mary told the Sunday Independent: 'We are married thirty-four years and the marriage could have worked. I wanted it to work. I wanted it to work. I really did, but she [Catherine Nevin] destroyed us.' Mary Kennedy said that Catherine would phone all the time asking for Mary's husband. 'I would say he's not here and she would ask "Where is he?" and I would say I don't know and she would ring back ten minutes later and ask all the same things again. It's been like this for years.'

Mary Kennedy also said she found it 'beneath my dignity to become involved ... But I'd love to know why Tom was down as next of kin, is she going to leave him all her money?'

8

THE ARKLOW JUDGE

When Judge Donnchadh Ó Buachalla took the stand in the Catherine Nevin trial, he denied ever having had an 'irregular affair' with the accused. The judge in the Wicklow–Wexford district for ten years made only a brief appearance in the Central Criminal Court, on 7 March 2000. He denied that he had ever stayed overnight on the premises or that he had ever had a set of keys to Jack White's, as Bernie Fleming and Liz Hudson, two members of staff, claimed, in evidence, they had been told by Catherine.

The judge gave his position to gardaí in a statement on 29 April 1996 in the Glenview Hotel. Judge Ó Buachalla said that he had known the late Tom Nevin and his wife for more than three years, and that he had been introduced to Jack White's pub and restaurant by Inspector Tom Kennedy. He said that he had developed connections with golf clubs in the Brittas Bay area, and that many members and guests of various clubs used Jack White's as the nearest hostelry, and also used its bed-and-breakfast facilities, and that some people used the shower and dining facilities after their games of golf as there was no club house at the nearby European Club. In fact, Jack White's was often seen as the unofficial 'nineteenth hole'. The judge said that he took part in prize-giving and was present at various functions for several golf clubs in Jack White's over the years. He said that Jack White's became a kind of halfway house for him on his travels and that he would call there on average two or three times a week. He said that he would often leave his car there when playing golf at local golf clubs. He said he had an excellent relationship with both the late Tom and his wife Catherine, and that they were both very hospitable and would regularly sit with him, depending upon which of them was not working at the counter. He said that there would be late nights from time to time, and that if he felt tired before driving, he would rest in the living room, have a shower and let himself out the front door and drive home. This happened on about three occasions, he said. He said that he never stayed overnight and that he had never had occasion to have a key to any part of the premises, and he had never had sight of any keys. He stated that he had no idea of the procedures for closing time or who locked the premises. It was common knowledge, he said, that Tom spent many hours late at night doing books and handling cash matters. Over time the judge said he became aware from the Nevins that they and many members of the local community felt great apprehension in relation to activities of certain members of the local gardaí. He said that Tom was greatly troubled by these ongoing matters, and that both Tom and Catherine firmly believed there was serious garda harassment over years and that it was futile to make complaints. He said that he last saw Tom on the night of Saturday, 15 March when he was in Jack White's with his wife and other family members for a meal; they ate in the conservatory between 8.15pm and 10.30pm and Tom came and joined them for about ten minutes.

◆　◆　◆

If the judge's attitude to Catherine Nevin was platonic, there is no doubt that she was infatuated by him. Debbie Boucher worked in Jack White's from 1992 to 1993. She told gardaí that she remembered that the judge, she thought his name was Ó Buachalla, used to call a lot to see Catherine, and that he and Catherine used to sit in the conservatory most of the time. She said that they used to get drunk a lot; that the judge, she thought, drank Harp, and would have wine with his dinner. She said that they used to sit up late, drinking, and if he got drunk, Catherine wouldn't let him drive home. Tom Nevin would ignore all this, she said, and he used to stay in the bar, playing darts or something like that. She said that she remembered one night that the judge slept in the Blue Room upstairs, the one with the sunbed, and that she had brought him up coffee and toast. Catherine told her to bring it up. She also said that sometimes, when they were drunk, Catherine used to massage the judge's back in front of everyone: that she'd sit up with the split in her dress wide open. The staff all thought this was funny. Catherine made a very big fuss of him. Sometimes the judge would have his wife, and a girl and a boy with him, for Sunday lunch.

Other members of staff also claim the judge stayed overnight in Jack White's, which he himself denied: Janey Murphy, who worked in the pub from 1987, told gardaí the judge had stayed over. She said that Catherine would make her iron the 'fancy sheets, they were lovely white ones with frills all over them, and that Catherine would say, "Make up the bed with the good sheets, the judge will be staying tonight".'

Eileen Byrne, who also worked in the pub, told gardaí that when the judge stayed overnight Catherine would tell her to leave out new tablets of soap and fresh towels for him in the morning.

Liz Hudson worked in the pub between 1991 and 1995. She told gardaí that towards the end of the summer of 1995 she went to work at 8.00am. She let herself in the hall door with the key. She was the first one in that morning. She had also been working the night before until closing time – around midnight or after. She said that Judge Ó Buachalla had come in earlier in the evening and that he and Catherine had been drinking in the crib area of the pub (a recessed area). They were still there when she went home. The next morning she went to pull back the curtains and in the crib area she saw a lot of wine bottles on the ground. They are Calvet or Chevalier half-bottles. Catherine always put the bottles on the floor in the crib.

◆　◆　◆

It was Ó Buachalla's issuing of a pub licence to Catherine Nevin, after she had been charged with Tom's murder, which hit the headlines and caused major concern with the general public. Catherine wished to renew the pub's licence in her sole name because her husband had been named on the previous licence as joint owner. But the Revenue Commissioner refused, informing her solicitor:

'Section 1 of the Licensing (Ireland) Act, 1833, only empowers the Revenue Commissioners to issue a renewed license "to the same persons and for the same houses as shall have been licensed in the year last immediately preceding." In my view the phrase "same persons" means exactly the same persons and not some of the same persons. The result of this is that the Revenue Commissioners have no power to issue a renewed licence in the sole name of a surviving joint tenant under section 1 of the 1833 Act, notwithstanding the fact that the surviving joint tenant was one of the licensees in the previous year.'

Judge Ó Buachalla then intervened, authorising Revenue on 13 June 1997:

'to delete from the said Licence the name of the said Thomas Nevin (now deceased) so that the same name shall stand in the sole name of Catherine Nevin.'

But Revenue again declined, claiming:

'Licenses cannot be transferred by arrangement between the parties but must be transferred by Order of the Court. The Revenue Commissioners will require a Court Order directing a transfer to the surviving joint tenant to enable them to issue a license in the sole name of the surviving joint tenant. ... I regret therefore that the Revenue Commissioners are not in a position to issue a license in your client's sole name without a Court Order. The authorisation of the District Judge dated the 13th June is not adequate and a Court order is required.'

The transfer to her sole name would therefore require a court hearing, which would give gardaí an opportunity to lodge objections and to raise the issue of the applicant's reputation – Catherine Nevin had already been charged with murder.

There was another complication. Tom Nevin's family had lodged a caveat to try to prevent Catherine from inheriting his property. As his spouse, she was entitled to everything, as Tom had died without making a valid will. Catherine was already joint owner of the pub and entitled to half its value. But if the property and the licence attached to it were in her name alone, she stood to make over half a million if the pub were sold.

On 29 September 1997, the day before the existing licence was due to lapse, Catherine applied for extensions to serve after hours. As was inevitable, the court was packed with reporters. Inspector Peter Finn of Gorey attended to lodge garda objections. Several grounds were put forward, including the imminent lapse of her basic seven-day licence, which would make the granting of extensions useless. Judge Donnchadh Ó Buachalla adjourned the hearing of the extension applications and informed Inspector Peter Finn, the District Court clerks and Catherine Nevin's solicitor that he was convening the court in his own chambers – in camera – ie, in the absence of the public and the press. There the judge made an order putting the licence into Catherine Nevin's sole name.

On 17 November 1997, the applications for the licence extensions that had been adjourned on 29 September came before Judge Ó Buachalla. They were again adjourned until 24 November, but not without a comment from the judge: 'It is of course clear that there was no transfer of the licence on the last day in court. It was a renewal, there was no objection from the Gardaí or any other party. The only outstanding matter now is the early morning licence.' Inspector Finn was again present in court and he asked the judge to repeat what he had said. The judge did so. The Irish Times reported the justice's comments on 18 November 1997, adding: 'It is understood [Ó Buachalla's] remarks were in reference to an earlier decision in Wexford District Court, where he granted a renewal of the pub licence. The licence had been in the name of Tom and Catherine Nevin and was renewed in the name of Catherine Nevin.'

After Catherine Nevin was found guilty of murder, Judge Ó Buachalla released a statement explaining why he had granted the order to put the licence in Catherine's sole name. The judge's statement read: 'A renewal certificate cannot be granted to a dead person and the licence had been in the joint names of Tom and Catherine Nevin. This difficulty was brought to the attention of the court in September 1997 and Inspector Finn of Gorey station attended at all discussions in relation to this matter. It became necessary to amend the existing licence so that a renewal could take place. When the matter came before the court at the annual licensing court there was no objection by the Gardaí to the renewal of the licence in the name of Catherine Nevin solely. This application was made in open court with Inspector Peter Finn confirming that the Gardaí had no objection.'

In fact, the issuing of the licence was a source of serious disquiet to Inspector Peter Finn, and an internal garda report, dated November 1997, shows that he had made not just one objection, he had made several. These were recorded by Superintendent Pat Flynn of Gorey in a report to the Crime and Investigation Branch in Dublin and to Assistant Commissioner Jim McHugh in Kilkenny. Flynn stated that Inspector Finn had been present in Wexford District Court on 29 September 1997 with the intention of renewing his objection to the three applications in respect of Jack White's, but that prior to the commencement of the court, Inspector Finn was requested to go to the judge's chambers. There, Catherine Nevin's solicitor made an application to the judge for a certificate, which would be submitted to the Customs and Excise, in support of a publican's licence being issued to Catherine Nevin in respect of Jack White's Licensed premises. Inspector Finn said he had no notice or indication of any sort that such an application would be made at the court, and so he informed the court. He objected to the application, informing the court that he was not on notice, the relevant notices had not been published in the newspapers, and that in his opinion the required application should be in respect of confirmation of transfer of the licence to Catherine Nevin. The judge adjourned the matter to 1.00pm on the same date. During the adjournment, Inspector Finn contacted Dan Prendeville, Higher Officer of Customs, Nenagh, Co. Tipperary, by phone and explained the situation that had developed to him. The Inspector also faxed a copy of the proposed order to Mr Prendeville. At 12.45pm Inspector Finn received a telephone call from Ms Etian Croasdell, Solicitor for the Customs and Excise, who stated that 'they would accept the order the judge was about to make.' When the application was called at 2.15pm the judge issued same. Again these proceedings were not heard in open court but in the judge's chambers. Judge Ó Buachalla issued the order as applied for despite the objections from Inspector Finn.

On 30 September 1997 a copy of the publican's licence issued to Catherine Nevin was handed in to Gorey Garda station. Following this handing in of the licence, further applications came before Arklow District Court, and on 20 October 1997 Superintendent J.P. Flynn himself objected to the application in respect of the General Exemption Order, as he felt that Catherine Nevin was not entitled to obtain such an order because of the statutory provisions dealing with such applications. As there was no objection in respect of the other two applications, they were granted by Judge Ó Buachalla.

Superintendent Flynn's document does not refer to a potential conflict of interest, which was widely discussed in the media, in respect of the judge hearing a friend's case. Commentators argued that the judge should not have become involved, as Catherine Nevin had been charged with murder and he, as a friend of the accused, was a potential witness at her trial. This is the reason cited by several Garda sources as to why Catherine Nevin was arrested for her husband's murder in Dublin, outside the jurisdiction of Judge Ó Buachalla. Ó Buachalla had also dined regularly with Catherine after she had been charged with murder. In their company was Tom Kennedy.

Also contained in the Garda file is confirmation that the judiciary were informed of garda disquiet about the licences. The Justice Minister was also made aware of the problem. Minister John O'Donoghue was told in 1997 of concerns over the transfer of the licence for the pub by Fine Gael Galway East deputy Ulick Burke, a personal friend of Tom Nevin's family. The family's hands were tied in opposing the renewal because they were afraid it would jeopardise the pending trial.

In any event, within three months of getting the licence from the judge, Catherine Nevin put Jack White's, of which she was now sole licensee, on the market. It was sold for over £670,000. This money is now frozen.

After Catherine Nevin was convicted of murder, the judge's actions relating to the licence resulted in the Minister for Justice launching a full-scale inquiry. There was major public interest and extensive media reports. The minister appointed Supreme Court Justice Frank Murphy to head the inquiry. Every detail of the application to put the licence in Catherine Nevin's sole name would be examined.

The preliminary hearing of the judicial inquiry sat in early July 2000 and it was decided that the evidence should be heard in public. From the outset the presiding judge, Supreme Court Justice Frank Murphy, divided the inquiry's workload into two modules. The first would deal with the handling of the Jack White's pub licence. The second would deal with the allegations about Judge Donnchadh Ó Buachalla's treatment of the Arklow gardaí Mick Murphy and Vincent Whelan.

The first stage involved three days of evidence, and they gave a foretaste of what was to come when the hearing would resume in September 2000. On the first day, 19 July, Judge Ó Buachalla made a statement explaining his actions: 'Having refused to deal with what was, clearly, an administrative problem which the acceptance of a death certificate would have resolved, Customs and Excise transferred this apparent difficulty to me, the licensing judge for the area. As a judge, I was obliged to resolve the question openly, honestly, logically, responsibly and in a manner which, legally, could not be impugned. This I did.'

Giving direct evidence, Catherine Nevin's solicitor, Donnchadh Lehane, said he had 'no idea' Judge Ó Buachalla and Catherine Nevin were such good friends when the order enabling the granting of the licence was made. On the second day of evidence Justice Frank Murphy described the fact that Catherine Nevin's solicitor had sought advice regarding the licence from Judge Ó Buachalla as 'unusual'. He was speaking during questions to Donnchadh Lehane concerning the meeting on 13 June 1997 in Judge Ó Buachalla's chambers. Justice Murphy asked why Lehane had not sought advice from a barrister instead: 'To seek the advice of the judge would in my view be unusual,' he said. Mr Lehane stressed that it was 'absolutely my idea' to ask Judge Ó Buachalla for advice. He also told Justice Murphy he didn't know why proceedings had taken place in chambers and not in open court. Earlier, responding to questions from Mr John Rogers SC, counsel for Judge Ó Buachalla, Mr Lehane said he did not find the holding of another meeting in Judge Ó Buachalla chambers in Wexford on 29 September 1997, at which six people were present, either surreal or peculiar and said he 'wouldn't be party to something like that'.

On the third day, Gorey District Court Clerk William Sexton told the inquiry that he had made notes in his diary for 25 September 1997 describing what he called 'outrageous' behaviour on the part of Judge Ó Buachalla. He recorded that when he and Garda Inspector Pat Flynn were having lunch in a pub that the judge had walked over to him and said, 'Ho, ho, ho – say no more, say no more.' Sexton also noted that when he had gone to where the judge was sitting to say goodbye after the lunch, the judge had said: 'Good luck, see you tomorrow,' and gestured with his hand to 'fuck off'.

John Rogers, counsel for Judge Ó Buachalla, accused Mr Sexton during his cross examination of 'tracking Judge Ó Buachalla's every move' – and he noted that in three of his diaries Mr Sexton had thirty different references to Judge Ó Buachalla.

The Minister for Justice, John O'Donoghue, said it was his intention to publish all the reports surrounding the case ordered by his Department, once Mr Justice Murphy had reported to him. In the meantime, members of staff who gave evidence at Catherine Nevin's murder trial were put on notice that they might be called in September to testify about the nature of Catherine Nevin's relationship with Judge Ó Buachalla.

Donnchadh Ó Buachalla was appointed to the Bench on 28 April 1989 by Charles Haughey's government, two weeks before the calling of a general election when Gerard Collins was the Minister for Justice. It was an unusual appointment, as Ó Buachalla had, when he was a solicitor, been declared bankrupt and was consequently unable to practise from 1973 to 1978.

Ó Buachalla had been in private practice when he started acting as a solicitor for a company called Invest of Ireland, based at Fitzwilliam Square, Dublin. This company was owned by the subsequently convicted fraudster, Tom Cawley, who had set up dozens of false investment companies. Invest of Ireland purported to offer mortgage funds, sourced from abroad, for commercial buildings, at a time when finance was difficult to get. Ó Buachalla was duped by Cawley, and he invested in the firm. When it fell through he was forced to declare bankruptcy. Another solicitor, the late Jonathon Phillip Toppin Brooks, a one-time partner in Beauchamps and a high flier, also paid the price for investing in one of Cawley's companies. Brooks committed suicide at his Annamoe home in County Wicklow, now owned by actor Daniel Day Lewis.

O'Buachalla was reinstated after he discharged his bankruptcy debt and went to work for his good friend, the solicitor Paddy Kevans, a director of Ed Farrell's Irish Permanent Building Society. Ed Farrell recently came to public attention at the Moriarty Tribunal for contributions to Fianna Fáil which ended up in Charles Haughey's personal account.

Ó Buachalla has a reputation as a very decent, affable man. However, it was rare enough for a bankrupt solicitor to be reinstated and later to be elevated to the Bench.

THE MEN WHO WERE ASKED
TO MURDER

Reconstruction

IMPORTANT INFORMATION

Catherine was sitting up in bed, astride Willie McClean, when the door opened. She turned her head to look over her shoulder, across her naked back. She knew from the fact that there was no light flooding in from the hallway that it was Tom. He always filled a doorframe. He was over 6ft in height, but with as much presence as a lamb.

She could feel Willie freeze at the sight of her husband, but Catherine didn't bat an eyelid. She had already explained to Willie that there was nothing between them anymore. Even now, Tom just said, 'Where are my keys, Catherine?' His voice was calm, not a trace of anger, nothing.

'They're on the kitchen table downstairs, and close the fucking door after you,' Catherine said. She had already warned him never to enter her room without knocking. The man in her bed was a Northern Protestant with important information she needed to get 'for the cause'.

Tom closed the door softly. Willie started to rant about how he couldn't believe Tom hadn't swung for him, another man in his bed – the Nevins were still sharing a bedroom at this stage. But Catherine knew that behind the façade, Willie was secretly chuffed. He must have thought he'd finally found himself the perfect set-up – a woman of means being kept by an estranged husband, whom Willie only needed to concern himself with on weekends. He had no idea what she wanted from him, at first.

They had met in the Red Cow Inn on Dublin's Naas Road in late 1984 or early 1985. He was at a table; she was at the bar – alone. He thought she was 'a good-looking bird', well dressed with big blond hair and lots of jewellery. She heard his Northern accent when he ordered a pint from the barman, and she struck up a conversation with him. She flashed her eyes, that way she had, when he started talking about his home town in Monaghan, and she showed him how impressed she was with all his talk of 'hookey' business – 'kiting cheques' and smuggling – by getting all tactile whenever he brought them up. Catherine knew they were going to become friends – at the very least. Then he mentioned the marches in Drumcree, and an incident in March 1974 when he was tortured because of the smuggling. The paramilitaries had ways of discouraging 'independents' who were not working for them – they cut their testicles. But not even the gardaí who arrived into the Accident and Emergency ward in Monaghan General Hospital had been able to crack him, and not even mutilation had stopped him continuing his business.

Catherine knew that she would have to find out more about Willie McClean. Catherine took Willie back to her place in Greenpark, Clondalkin, beside the Green Isle Hotel. When she told him he was an amazing lover, he replied that his nickname up North was 'The Blonde Bombshell' because of all the women he'd had. She told him straight off that she was married, but explained that she and Tom led separate lives.

For the first year, Willie couldn't get enough of 'Cathy'. She knew the way to keep him was by being sex-mad. When she moved with her husband to Jack White's in May 1986, Willie followed, even helping move the furniture – he kept a lorry for his skip-removal business, working the building sites. For the first two or three months, he stayed nearly every weekend in Jack White's. He'd do a bit of work behind the bar – not for the money, mind, 'Cathy' would never stoop to paying him nor he to taking it.

Sometimes, when she needed to get away from Tom, she took him to a flat in a house in Rialto, Dublin. She told him a lot of things. About the hysterectomy she had had in England before she married Tom, which Tom never knew about. About the .38 revolver she always carried with her and the shotgun under her bed. Sometimes she even told him she loved him.

He was at the pub's official opening, but he kept to himself. He was thinking about the way Catherine could make you feel like you had disappeared when somebody better came along.

He never did have the loyalist paramilitary friends she wanted him to brief her about. No matter how many times she brought up the subject, he was not going to play that game. He kept telling her his business was waste disposal, he had a skip, end of story. After a year and a half, he had had enough of her.

But she wouldn't let him go. Her job wasn't done. A few times he tried to bring up the subject of ending the relationship, but she always talked him around.

Then, one weekend, he arrived into the pub with a woman. It was his way of letting Catherine know loud and clear that it was over between them. He knew how possessive she was. But he didn't know how crazy she'd be. He didn't think she'd threaten to shoot him. She threw them both out of the pub.

Willie called to Jack White's again, four years later, some time early in 1990 or so. He was curious – but he was also armed with another woman. It didn't stop 'Cathy' from cornering him on the way to the toilet and asking for his phone number. He gave her the name of his local; no way would he give her his home number, knowing what she was capable of. He made sure to tell her again: 'Our day is gone, Cathy.'

But by 1990, Catherine wanted Willie for himself, not for what he knew. She sent free slices of Christmas cake over to him and his girlfriend, to show him how calm she was about everything. Still, she made sure she took down the registration number of the car he was driving. By now she had a lot of influence with the guards. You could find out a lot from a person's car reg.; you never knew when it might come in handy. She kept the scrap of paper with DIL 5206 in her bedside locker.

9

WILLIE McCLEAN

On 18 May 1996, Jack White's was searched. Among the items seized was a scrap of paper from Catherine Nevin's bedside locker. Scribbled across it was 'DIL 5206'. Insignificant though it seemed, the item would end up as Exhibit Number 3 in the Catherine Nevin murder trial. DIL 5206 turned out to be a Northern-registered Opel Kadett. Tracking its owner led Sergeant Joe O'Hara of Gorey station to Harold's Cross Road in Dublin, the home of Willie McClean, one of the state's three main witnesses in the case against Catherine Nevin. It came as no surprise to McClean that a guard was on his doorstep inquiring about the murder in Jack White's. Nor was it a surprise to Sergeant O'Hara that McClean had not come forward of his own free will. Willie McClean likes to make a quick buck: the last thing he needed was the law on his back, watching his every move.

McClean, from Monaghan, has three criminal convictions, two for deception (fraud) in the North. He used a cheque to buy a Land Rover, without the funds to meet it in the bank. He was charged with theft by deception in Omagh City Court, he says, in '1972 or 1973' and, on appeal, a three-month sentence handed down was affirmed – but he fled. He admitted during the Catherine Nevin murder trial that technically he probably still is a wanted man in the North. He was also bound over to the peace for bouncing a cheque in the South in the late 1980s.

McClean was the first to admit to Sergeant O'Hara that he dabbles in 'hookey business' – smuggling spirits and the like across the border – and in 'kiting cheques'. But he is not a killer. He told O'Hara that he had had an eighteen-month affair with Catherine Nevin, which he ended around September 1986 because she was too 'possessive'. A chance call into Jack White's four years later resulted in Catherine asking for his phone number. She rang him at his local pub, the Irish House, and asked him to visit her in St Vincent's Hospital. For old times' sake he called in to see how she was. When he sat on her hospital bed, she made overtures, asking him to kill her husband for £20,000.

In a statement to gardaí, McClean described exactly how the proposal came about: 'I would say about 1990 myself and my present girlfriend were out for a drive and we decided to call in to Jack White's for a jar. Catherine was there and she spoke to us. She was chatty enough. That day I was driving DIL 5206, an Opel Kadett. I had parked the car outside the pub. That is the only time ever that our car was outside the pub. We had about four or five jars and left. I didn't have any contact with Catherine Nevin until about six to eight months later. She had asked me if I had a telephone number. I told her if she wanted to contact me she could ring me in the Irish House pub, in Harold's Cross. Catherine Nevin rang me at the Irish House pub, I can't remember exactly when. She rang me from St Vincent's Private Hospital, it was about evening time. She asked me to call out to the hospital to see her. She told me she was in hospital for some kind of heart complaint. I called out to St Vincent's Private Hospital the next day. She was in a private room. Catherine was very chatty and friendly. Catherine said she still loved me and wanted to start the affair again. It was a non starter with me anyway. I told her I didn't want to go again. She went on a bit about getting back together. Suddenly she asked me to do something for her. She said, "There is £20,000 there to get rid of Tom, you and I could get back together." I was shocked and said, "Fuck off, Catherine." I said, "Where would this happen?" Catherine said, "Get him going to the bank or at the flats." She said, "You would have the contacts." I was shocked and said no fucking way, got up and walked out. I left the hospital.'

As in the case of Gerry Heapes, one of the other men whom Catherine solicited to murder her husband (see Chapter 11), the proposal did not signal an end to the visits to Jack White's. 'The next time I saw Catherine Nevin was Patrick's Day 1993. I was on my way to Rosslare. I was on the way to Switzerland driving a Mercedes truck. I called into Jack White's that day with my nephew. We had a few drinks. Catherine was there and she spoke to me, she was friendly and just had a chat. She did not mention anything about what we spoke about in the hospital. We called in on the way back but Catherine was not there, we had a meal and left.'

When he took the stand on 24 February 2000, Willie McClean was a reluctant witness. His experience of the law had never been pleasant. When he was asked about the nature of his relationship with Catherine, he turned and looked her in the eye before he declared: 'sexual'.

But when Catherine's lawyers reduced their history to just a meeting she had with the furniture removal man, who was a friend of her husband's, on the day she moved to Wicklow, he retaliated. Not only was he her lover, he made clear, but he was also an unpaid worker in the bar, receiving 'payment in kindness'.

'My husband was very fussy about who worked behind the bar,' Nevin stated. If McClean was at the pub's opening night, she didn't remember him, she said.

McClean said he could prove that he had worked in Jack White's and was at the pub opening. Ask the customer 'with a deformed hand' who drank at the bar, he said, referring to Paddy Doyle, the fisherman. The guards approached Doyle, who remembered Willie, but vaguely, and he could not remember his name. But McClean also said he remembered serving members of the gardaí while behind the bar. Sergeant Des Kidney, a retired guard, was invited to the pub's opening night and did remember being served by Willie McClean. But Kidney's evidence was never admitted as rebuttal evidence in court.

Kidney's statement reads: 'I can recall the following morning I was at home at about 10.30am when Catherine Nevin called to my home. She was accompanied by a man whom I now know to be Willie McClean ... I remember Willie McClean being there on several weekends. He used to serve there behind the bar and served me drink several times. He was there on and off during weekends for a few months after the Nevins bought the pub. Willie McClean appeared to be friendly with Catherine Nevin. I also recall that Willie McClean stayed there at Jack White's constantly for about two weeks. I remember Willie McClean telling me at the time that he was involved in skip hire business.'

Kidney also claimed: 'I can recall at the time that Paddy Doyle was a regular drinker at Jack White's at the time. He was involved in a fishing boat and has only one arm. He lost the arm in a fishing-boat accident.'

Willie McClean described Tom Nevin as 'a nice, quiet man'. Nevin had seen him in bed with Catherine, but never mentioned it afterwards. McClean never saw Tom being violent towards Catherine, and he also never saw any expression of matrimonial relations between the two. He said he saw no prominent Republicans like Joe Cahill at the opening.

When in the stand, McClean was cross-examined by Catherine Nevin's Junior Counsel, Paul Burns, because Nevin's barrister, like McClean, is from Monaghan and their fathers would have known each other (Paddy McEntee's father was a

Above: Tom and Catherine Nevin on their wedding day, 13 January 1976.

Right: Catherine's publicity shot for her modelling agency, and, *inset*, the letter-head from her business notepaper.

FROM
THE CATHERINE SCULLY MODEL AGENCY
AND BEAUTY GROOMING SCHOOL
6 Mayfield Road,
Rialto,
Dublin 8.

The State's three main witnesses in the Catherine Nevin trial: *left* Willie McClean, *above* John Jones, *below* Gerry Heapes.

Right: Inspector Tom Kennedy (retired).

Below: Judge Donnchadh Ó Buachalla.

The murder scene is preserved at Jack White's on 19 March 1996.

Above: Tom Nevin's brothers carry his coffin.

Left: Catherine clutching a rose during Tom's funeral.

Reporters were prevented from mentioning Catherine's appearance during the trial, but it was obvious that she flourished under the glare of the cameras.

Top: Catherine sniffles when leaving the court.

Above: She adjusts her hair as her brother drives her to court.

Left: She had her hair done every morning before court.

Left: Judge Mella Carroll, who heard the case.

Above: Catherine's legal team –
Paddy McEntee SC (*right*) and Paul Byrnes.

Former staff members of Jack White's who were witnesses at the trial –
left Liz Hudson and *right* Janey Murphy.

Former staff members of Jack White's who were witnesses at the trial –
left Caroline Strahan and *right* Eileen Byrne.

Catherine Nevin is led to the prison van by Mountjoy wardens
after being found guilty of murder and sentenced to prison.

dentist in Monaghan).

Burns called McClean a conman and a deceiver. Burns quoted the garda notes on Gerry Heapes's first statement, in which he referred to McClean as an 'embezzler'. He said McClean would have to have had paramilitary protection to be able to smuggle anything across the Monaghan border route. Burns later retracted this allegation and apologised to the court. The State Prosecutor, Peter Charleton SC, warned that such comments made it extremely difficult for someone like Willie McClean to face people at home. Charleton said if such statements were allowed to stay on the record it would put witnesses off coming forward to give evidence.

It did McClean no favours either when, in his summing up, McEntee described him as 'lacking in candour' and 'living off his wits'. Catherine also ripped him apart when she took the stand, calling him a counterfeiter. 'I only know what my husband told me,' she said, 'he said he had plates and was into making £20 notes.' The State denied this.

But Judge Mella Carroll made no apologies for his background. In summing up, she referred to the way the state had presented the three main witnesses 'as they are with all their faults'. She reminded the jury that the 'similar fact' evidence in McClean's case was thin because Catherine had not proposed Tom be killed during a bank-holiday weekend or robbery, but that [McClean] had supplied evidence of motive.

After everything that was said about him in court, it is no wonder that someone like Willie McClean hadn't come forward to help gardaí of his own volition.

10

JOHN JONES

John Jones was born on 12 November 1944. In the 1980s he ran a TV rentals shop called Channel Vision on Church Street in Finglas – at a time when there was a recession and many families could still afford only to rent their TV. It hired out around 200 television sets with weekly payments. In court, Pat Russell described it as consisting of the entire first floor, No. 2a. There were six rooms in all. At the top of the stairs were two doors. One led to the TV shop, which had a sales room, a repair room and two storage rooms. The other led to the Sinn Féin advice centre – Jones was the Chair of the local Sinn Féin cumann. The advice centre consisted of two rooms. One was a clinic for members of the public, and the other a meeting room for members – like Gerry Heapes, Tommy Thompson and Pat Russell. They would meet there, and also make hankies and crosses to sell in pubs to raise funds.

Jones's partner in the TV business was Dessie Ellis. Ellis's job was to fix the broken TV sets. The rental business had a turnover of around £50,000 a year, until Ellis was extradited in 1990 to Britain in connection with bomb-making charges relating to 1982–84. After Ellis's extradition, Jones's workload in the TV shop doubled, so Pat Russell took over as Chair of the cumann.

But Jones still held the post when he first met Catherine Nevin in 1984–85, when she came in to the advice centre. She claimed in court that she told him that she wanted to buy or lease a pub and she claimed that she had been recommended by a Sinn Féin councillor, Christy Burke. Jones claimed in court that he told her it was not something the party could do anything about. In the event, Catherine and Tom Nevin did manage to get the lease on The Barry House pub, which had a very troubled history and which was about to re-open after a riot in 1983.

During the Nevins' time in The Barry House, Catherine encouraged Jones to organise Sinn Féin meetings in the pub. Members sold copies of An Phoblacht and both Catherine and Tom attended Sinn Féin rallies. She also gave Jones business, renting a sound system and two TVs from him.

Her requests to Jones to have him kill her husband did not begin until around six years later, 1989–90, when the Nevins had moved to Jack White's. She again called in to the advice centre.

'It was obvious that there was something on her mind other than whatever conversation we were having,' Jones explained when giving a deposition of his evidence to the District Court on 28 July 1998 in relation to the Catherine Nevin trial. He continued: 'She was speaking about everything except the obvious thing that was on her mind. So finally she said to me, "I have a proposition for you." And I said, "Go ahead." I didn't know what was going to come out. And she said, "I want you to get the IRA to shoot my husband … in what would look like a robbery".'

Jones said he was 'taken aback. I wasn't sure if it was her sense of humour or what the hell it was.' Weeks later, Catherine returned to the advice centre and asked Jones if he had thought about her proposition. She went into more detail. Jones related that she said: 'There would be an attempted – what would look like a robbery – following a bank-holiday weekend [and] she would ensure that there would be a considerable amount – £25,000 or £23,000 – and she would ensure that; Tom would normally – after the bank-holiday weekend, I think it was a Tuesday or a Wednesday – he would travel to a bank in Dublin and normally have a young barman [with him]. And she said she would ensure that there was no one with him at the time. The IRA would stage the robbery … en-route.'

Jones said he gave her a flat refusal. He said, 'How she could expect volunteers of Óglaigh na hÉireann to act in such a fashion baffles me.' But he did report her 'proposition' back to two senior members of the cumann. 'First they said I had been mistaken about what was said, she was obviously pulling my leg, this was a black joke – or that was one train of thought. The other one was that there was something more sinister going on, not only herself but Tom. We weren't sure where they were coming from or what was happening.' Jones and his co-party members believed that Catherine might even be a garda plant sent to infiltrate the organisation and set them up.

On several other occasions, Catherine asked if he had thought any more about the proposition. She called to his home in Balbriggan, where he had moved from Finglas in 1982. Catherine claimed she was passing anyway, having bought meat in Dundalk for the pub. On one occasion she actually left meat with him as a present.

She would talk first about her plans for Jack White's. 'She was quite enthusiastic about it. It was the main auto route which is now being developed which is the main land route between ourselves and Europe … She told me that there was a vast amount of money available because it was en route and she was making it a major truck stop for truckers going to the ferry ports and developing a restaurant.'

But Catherine's ambition was always premised on getting rid of Tom, and that was the real reason for her house calls. In total, her propositions to John Jones numbered six or seven, and spanned a year or a year and a half.

One time she called to him in the advice centre wearing black glasses and bandages on her wrists, claiming Tom had hit her.

When Tom Nevin was murdered, Jones said his initial reaction was: 'God, she's gone ahead and done it.' He rang Pat Russell, and told him that 'I was going to the guards with what information I had.'

Jones further said in evidence in court that Russell advised him not to in case the gardaí 'put him in the frame'. Jones also said he was sick of the treatment he had got from Special Branch over the years because he was a Republican. Jones said Pat Russell told him to wait until the gardaí got in touch with him.

The gardaí did track Jones down, after finding his phone number on one of several scraps of paper in Catherine's bedside locker, during the search of Jack White's. The television rental business was gone and he was working in Dublin Airport, driving a bus bringing passengers to and from the car parks to the airport terminal. Later, he left this to work in an alarm-installation business.

He was not surprised to see them 'because I knew that Catherine Nevin had done it, that's why I phoned Mr Russell … It was blatantly clear to me that she had done it,' he said. The detectives asked Jones if he knew Catherine Nevin. He answered yes. The conversation was brief because Jones was working. They told him they'd be in touch. They called to see him a second time, and again the conversation lasted just minutes. The next time the detectives made contact they phoned his home and organised to meet him in the local Garda station. The reason he was not immediately forthcoming with what he knew was because: 'I had to consider the ramifications to my family – which I find to my cost are happening, because of the media and the effect on the business.'

In Balbriggan Garda station in July 1996, Jones gave gardaí

the following statement:

'I am a member of Sinn Féin. Between the years 1980 or 1990 or so, I had a TV Repair shop known as Channel Vision Ltd at 2A Church Street, Finglas. There were two rooms at the back of the shop which I used as an advice centre for Sinn Féin. This was run by a man named Tommy Thompson, RIP, and myself. Around 1984 a woman whom I now know to be Catherine Nevin called to the advice centre. She stated that she had been referred by a prominent City Councillor. I later checked with this man and he stated he couldn't recall anybody like that. Her query was in relation to pubs available in the area. This I took to mean either buy or lease. This was a very unusual request at Sinn Féin advice centre and my initial reaction was one of suspicion. I wasn't able to assist her. Sometime later I heard that she had taken over The Barry House in Finglas. She continued her association with the advice centre. She also introduced me to her husband Tom. They made the pub available to us to run functions and sell An Phoblacht. She developed a close relationship with certain members of the cumann. I am aware that they tried to buy the pub while they were there but they were prevented from doing so over some disagreement with the landlord. She appeared to me to be trying to curry favour with certain members of the cumann. She attended rallies with Tom in Finglas. These were political rallies. Sometime later, possibly 1986, they moved to Jack White's in Wicklow. She still called into the advice centre possibly once a month. This was when she stated that she was attending the Mater Hospital getting blood treatment or visiting their flats in the city. She later started calling to my house in Balbriggan. On these occasions she stated that she was returning from Dundalk where she was collecting meat for the pub. On one occasion she even left in a present of some meat. I still retained certain suspicion of her. Sometime, I believe in 1989, Catherine called to the advice centre and spoke to me in private. She said that she had a proposition that we might be interested in. She said that she wanted us to stage a robbery and in the course of the robbery Tom was to be killed. She said the plan was that it would be arranged for the Tuesday following the Bank Holiday weekend. She said the hit would take place when Tom was (travelling) en route to the bank. She said that the amount he would be carrying would be in the region of £25,000. This money would be for us. She said that Tom went to the Bank with a member of the staff normally but she could arrange that Tom was travelling alone. She said the bank was in Rathmines, Rathgar or somewhere on the Southside. I didn't entertain this suggestion at all. I told her that we were not into that type of thing. I felt it my duty to report this approach to more senior members of the organisation. I got in touch with them sometime the same day and informed them of this. There were two members of the organisation at this meeting. They concurred with my opinion that this wasn't something we should be getting involved in. She approached me with this on a number of other occasions and eventually I had to tell her that I didn't want the subject brought up again, ever. She never mentioned this to me again. I believe the last time she asked me was about one year after the initial approach. Subsequently, I am aware that she approached two other members of the organisation with a similar proposition. These approaches took place before I left Finglas. The last time I saw her was when she called to my home about two or three years ago. I can recall an occasion either before or after she made the initial proposition when she called to the advice centre. She had bandages on both wrists and hands and she had a black eye which she shielded with sunglasses. She stated that Tom had beaten her up. She said that the Tom we knew wasn't the same Tom that she knew after the pub closed at night time. She said that the Guards that visited the pub and drank with Tom were fooled the same way also. I saw the report of the murder on the TV later on the day it happened. I immediately suspected that I knew what had probably happened. Over the following days, I began to have a guilty conscience about this knowledge. I rang up a Sinn Féin colleague and told him that I was thinking of going to the Gardaí about the matter. I didn't want to see her getting away with that. I was advised not to go as it may be putting myself in the frame.'

Jones came back to gardaí and made a second statement: 'I wish to add that the only time I can be sure that Catherine Nevin mentioned being assaulted by Tom Nevin was the day she came into the advice centre with her hands and wrists bandaged and wearing the sunglasses to cover her black eye. She may have mentioned it in passing at other times but I cannot recall it at this time. On that day she came into the advice centre and sat across the table from me. She took off her glasses and said, "What do you think of that?", showing her black eye. I could have said, "How did it happen?" or something like that. She then went on to tell me that Tom had beat her. It was at this stage she said that "He is not the type of guy ye think he is and the Guards that drink with him would be surprised by it too." She went on to say that she had to put up with the effects of Tom's drinking after the pub closed its doors at night. During our conversation she also told me about the big plans she had for the premises at Jack White's. She mentioned a truck overnight stop. She mentioned that there was EC grants for this. She mentioned that she was being advised by her solicitor. When she put the proposition to me that she wanted her husband Tom Nevin killed during the course of the robbery and on other discussions with her, it was apparent to me the reason she wanted him killed was to take full control of the Business. She mentioned the proposition to kill Tom Nevin to me on at least six other occasions at intervals over the next 12 months. The way she would introduce it was during the course of general conversation, she would say, "By the way, did you think any more about my proposition?"

These propositions were always mentioned in either the advice centre or the pub across the road where I would go for a coffee with her, if she had looked for me in the advice centre and I wasn't there. When she mentioned the proposition I knew that it was the proposition to kill Tom Nevin in the staged robbery. She visited my home on about five or six times. On at least one of the occasions I wasn't there and she just left a message that she had called. Having been made the proposition by Catherine Nevin initially, I discussed the matter with two persons, one of whom was Pat Russell, another member of the local cumann. The second man was a prominent member of the organisation whom I do not wish to name. Having heard about the murder, I contacted Pat Russell about my concerns on the matter. I told him I was going to the Guards about the matter.'

Jones gave a third statement about the night in question: 'On the night of the 18th of March 1996 morning of the 19.3.1996 I cannot recall exactly where I was, I will check with my work place to establish if I was working or not. In relation to the time Mrs Catherine Nevin called to the advice centre (Sinn Féin) in Finglas that she had a black eye and her wrists bandaged – she stated that she had been assaulted by her husband Tom Nevin and had attended the Mater Private Hospital. I cannot say exactly when this was but it was definitely during her time in Jack White's. As close as I can come to the actual time is to say it was between 1986 and 1989.'

During his deposition to the District Court, Jones had also been asked to name the two senior members of the cumann he claimed he told at the time about Catherine Nevin's requests. He identified one as Pat Russell, but said that he could not recall the name of the other. Judge Mary Malone told him: 'You should give the name of the person you spoke to.' Jones replied: 'Just a question to yourself. If I am not at liberty to give the name, that's the scenario I am raising.' The judge said, 'You either know the name or you don't know the name', and Jones said he did not know the name.

It emerged in the course of the deposition hearing that Jones had not been given State immunity, and that he had given a statement of his own volition.

In the Central Criminal Court on 29 February 2000, Catherine's barrister, Paddy McEntee SC, also asked him to name the two senior members of the cumann he claimed he told at the time about Catherine Nevin's requests. Jones replied that one was Pat Russell, a university student at the time, 'very well educated and an enthusiastic worker'. He said he could not recall the identity of the other, though he had told gardaí that 'the second man was a prominent member of the organisation whom I do not wish to name.'

He also said that he had not relayed the message to the IRA, as Catherine requested, as he wouldn't know how to get in touch with the IRA even if he wanted to. When questioned by Paddy McEntee SC about this, he said he did not know Gerry Heapes's background, just that he was a Republican from Finglas.

Paddy McEntee SC asked Jones why he had waited so long before telling Catherine once and for all not to mention the subject again. Jones said that every time she brought up killing Tom he told her he wanted nothing to do with it, but that he couldn't control her walking into the advice centre.

McEntee asked him why he didn't tell her to 'get out of the building and never darken it again'. He asked why he had not gone to Jack White's pub and told her never to set foot in the advice centre again? And he asked why Jones had not 'lifted the phone' to ring Jack White's and warn her husband?

Jones said when Tom Nevin was murdered he had again contacted Pat Russell. 'When Catherine Nevin murdered Tom Nevin I got in touch with Pat Russell and told him I was coming to the police with the information that Catherine Nevin had propositioned me. That I felt it was my duty.' Jones said Russell advised him that the gardaí would, no doubt, be in touch with him and 'I shouldn't get involved because the Guards had been so heavy on me … because of my reputation as an active Republican, the guards would be more than happy to make trouble for me.' He explained how they would sit outside, making running a business embarrassing. 'To be honest,' he said, 'from the amount of contact I had with Catherine Nevin, if the Gardaí were doing half their duty they would have arrived at my door.'

Jones was in Jack White's twice between 1986 and 1989, but he did not visit again after Catherine asked him to have Tom killed. He said he knew nothing about Catherine's claim that he had called at Jack White's to collect a cheque for £1,200 for VAT.

McEntee put it to him that Catherine had never asked him to have her husband killed. Jones replied: 'Mr McEntee, I would expect you to say that, you're defending the woman, but I'm telling you she sat in front of me and asked me to get the IRA to kill her husband and no talking or bluster can change that.'

McEntee referred to a previous criminal conviction, from 18 November 1988, when Jones had received a three-year suspended sentence and was ordered to pay £3,000 to an insurance company and £500 to a car owner for handling stolen goods. He claimed he did not know the car was stolen when he bought it. In his evidence, Jones said: 'I purchased a car from an ad in a newspaper 23 years ago and drove it for a while and put it in the garage when the numbers did not match. I considered how to get rid of it and pushed it out the driveway and two hours later branch men arrived at my door. I employed the services of a very prominent barrister to fight the case because it was a genuine case and because when someone has a Republican background the gardaí can make it extremely difficult.' By an amazing coincidence, his barrister had been Paddy McEntee SC.

11

GERRY HEAPES

Gerry Heapes was born on 28 May 1950 and grew up in Finglas on Dublin's northside. He was working as a porter in Jervis Street Hospital when, on 26 November 1977, he carried out an armed robbery on Leyden's Cash and Carry in Richmond Road. Heapes was a member of the Provisional IRA. He was sentenced on 10 December 1977 to ten years' imprisonment. He was defended by Paddy McEntee SC, whom he met again twenty-three years later, but on the opposite side, at Catherine Nevin's trial.

Heapes served his time on the Provo wings E2, E3, E4 of Portlaoise prison and was released in April 1985. He joined the Jack McCabe cumann of Sinn Féin in Finglas in August of that year. Sinn Féin held a fundraiser for him in The Castle, Tubercross, to help him get back on his feet: £255 was raised. Heapes was unemployed and spent the days working in the office behind the advice centre tracing Republican prints onto hankies, which were sold to cumainn in America.

It was here that he first met Catherine Nevin, who was always 'popping in' to the advice centre. After she left Finglas and moved to Jack White's in 1986, she continued to call into The Barry House, to visit old customers and also to call in to the centre.

She invited Heapes to the opening of Jack White's. He said Catherine Nevin spoke to his wife and himself to point out who was who. 'She said, "That's a judge, that's an inspector, that's a load of farmers."' In 1989, Catherine came looking for Heapes in Finglas. Heapes had left Sinn Féin in 1988 because 'we were in a lot of debt and I had given the best part of 20 years to the cause. I reckoned I had to give time to the five kids and the wife.' He had been in prison when his youngest child was born. 'I hadn't got to hold that child for eight years.' There was a big turnover of members because of the 'hassle from Special Branch'. But he continued to go to funerals of former inmates and associates.

During the search of Jack White's, following Tom Nevin's murder, the guards seized a phone book they found there. But by then, Catherine had scribbled over Heapes's name and number on both the front and back of the page. Forensic experts were able to lift the ink and read the name underneath. It became Exhibit Number 5 in the case against her.

When first arrested at the end of July 1996, Heapes was brought to Enniscorthy Garda station where he was held for forty-eight hours. He would not cooperate with investigators. However, the following day, he contacted gardaí to say he was now prepared to make a statement. He explained the reason for this change of heart to Paddy McEntee SC: 'I had been held for two days. When I went home, I seen the state of my wife and family. I had no intention of making any statement. My wife said, "If you know anything, will you tell them?" When I seen the state of her I talked to the police. They writ it down. I went in and said what I had to say.'

Heapes's statement took three hours to complete. He didn't sign it at the time, but later confirmed the substance of it in the course of giving his deposition in the District Court. It reads:

'I first met Catherine Nevin in the Sinn Féin advice centre in 1985. This is the Sinn Féin office in Finglas. I was introduced to her by members of Sinn Féin. She was a regular visitor to the centre and I met her frequently. I got an invitation for myself and my wife to attend the official opening of Jack White's Inn. Myself and my wife attended the opening and stayed for two nights. At the opening I was introduced to Willie McClean. He was at the time working there. I found out later that Willie McClean and Catherine were having an affair. Some years after I first met Catherine Nevin she approached me in Finglas one day and asked me to go for a drive with her. Catherine was at that time driving a large white-coloured car. She drove me to the Phoenix Park. She told me that she was having trouble with her husband. I knew her husband Tom Nevin personally. She said that he was making her life hell. She said that he was beating her up and that he was having affairs. She also said that the money that was used to buy Jack White's Inn had been her money and that he gave her no money. I found that very hard to believe because I knew Tom and whenever I saw Catherine she always had plenty of gold jewellery and money and was often just after returning from holiday and was very well tanned. She turned around asked me would I get rid of Tom. She said she wanted him shot dead. I was kind of taken aback when she said it. I thought it was a wind-up. I said to her that costs money. She started about that on a bank holiday weekend he would be carrying between £20,000 and £25,000 cash. I said £25,000 is not worth a person's life. At this stage I was thinking that this wasn't a wind-up and that this woman was serious. I said to her leave it with me and get back to me in a week or so. I went and told people of what I had been propositioned. These people thought it was a wind-up, but if she came back I was told to get as much detail off her and report back. A few weeks after the first meeting she approached me again and brought me back to the Phoenix Park. She asked me did I think about what she had asked me. I said that nobody would do it for that kind of money. She said, "Well, what are you talking about?" (meaning money). I said that there would have to be more money because there would have to be cars and motorbikes and guns bought and they would have to be untraceable. She said that there was a double insurance policy on Tom's life and that she would pay after it had been collected. I said to her that no one would do a murder unless they got the money up front. I told her to come back to me if she could come up with the money. I reported all this back to other people. They told me to keep in contact with her and report back to them. About 2 or 3 weeks later Catherine Nevin approached me again and we went back to the Phoenix Park, where she told me that she thought that she had resolved the problem about the money. She said that she reckoned that she could skim money out of Jack White's each week and ... [she] would open an account in her maiden name and not tell Tom. I said to her to get back to me when there is money in the account. Some four or five weeks later she approached me again and once more we went to the Phoenix Park. She took out from her purse a bank book with lodgements in it. I can't remember the amount or the name of the bank but she showed me a name on the book which she said was her maiden name. I can't remember what the name was. When she showed me the bank book I realised that Catherine Nevin was serious about having her husband killed. I asked her what was the best way to go about it. She asked me was I in a hurry and I said no. She brought me up to a house off the South Circular Road. This house is in a row of terraced houses, on the right hand side of the road as you turn right off the South Circular Road when driving towards James Hospital Rialto entrance. She stopped outside a house and said that this is Tom's first stop after he leaves Jack White's pub. He usually had a barman or handyman that worked in Jack White's with him. She said that the barman would go in and collect the rent from the two houses and he would give the money to Tom. She said that this would be the perfect place to do him. I said that the streets were too small and there were too many cars parked on them: we couldn't sit in a car waiting for Tom as we would be noticed. She said to me that she would arrange to get keys for the front door of the house and that we could wait inside the hall for him as the apartments would all be empty as the people would all be at work by the time Tom arrived. With the narrow doorway, small garden with iron railings and gate, by the time we got past, your man Tom would be gone. I said to her that you better come up with a better idea. We left it at that and I reported back and they were taking it very seriously at this stage. About three days after this meeting we met again. Catherine took me on a drive from their flats off the South Circular Road. We travelled from the South Circular Road into Islandbridge and into the Phoenix Park and as we were driving she told me that this was the route that Tom took and that he drove fast, at around 70mph, all the time to make the bank before it closed for lunch and that if he missed the bank at lunchtime he would drive onto Clonee and he would park directly outside the window of the Grasshopper pub. He would leave the takings of Jack White's in the boot of the car with the alarm on and he would watch the car while he was having lunch. When he was finished lunch he would head back towards Blanchardstown and stop at Keepak in Clonee to collect meat for the pub. Catherine and I travelled the exact route from the flats to Clonee that Tom travelled every Monday or, in the case of a bank holiday weekend, on a Tuesday. While we were outside the Grasshopper pub in Clonee, Catherine said that this was the perfect place to do him. Then she drove me back to the Phoenix Park and brought me down a slip road near Wellington Monument. She stopped the car and she showed me the view of Islandbridge. From this point you could see the road at Islandbridge coming from the direction of their flats. She said that from this point we could see Tom's car crossing the bridge and follow it and that we could time his arrival there and his journey from there. We then discussed money. We had agreed £35,000. That was £10,000 up front and £25,000 in takings. I said leave it with me for a few weeks until I time Tom on his runs. I reported back again from the impression I got then, knowing how serious the matter was that action would be taken to stop the matter, either by telling Tom or calling Catherine in. But a couple of days later she arrived out in Finglas and brought me for a drive to the Grasshopper pub in Clonee. We parked on the opposite side from the pub. She said she was thinking over the last couple of days, that she thought that she hadn't got a good alibi, and she said that if she was with Tom she would make sure that he would miss the bank for lunchtime, and would have to go to the Grasshopper pub for lunch with the money. That would give her a perfect alibi by being with him. I said to her that it would be too dangerous for her. If someone was being shot there was no telling where the bullets might go. Catherine said all the better if she was wounded, that she would really look the part of the grieving widow. I asked her how I was to get the money out of the boot of the car, could she get me a spare key. She said that Tom would have the keys in his hand coming out of the pub and to take them off him – as he wouldn't be able to do anything as he would be dead. Catherine also stated that she would make sure that Tom left the Grasshopper pub first. At this meeting Catherine said that the coming St Patrick's day weekend would be the ideal time to do it. I said that it was too short of notice as there was too much work to be done to set it up. I asked her was she sure about the takings that it was the amount. Catherine said that on a bank holiday weekend the takings from the pub are left in the Garda Station in Wicklow each night over the weekend. I think it was Wicklow Station she said. Tom would collect the takings there on the Tuesday morning on his way to Dublin. She said that there were two Gardaí who kept the money for them in their lockers. I went back and reported the details of this meeting with Catherine and I was told not to worry that something was being done straight away. A few days later I heard that some people had either gone out to Catherine at Jack White's or had brought her to Dublin and told her that they knew what she was up to and that it was over and if they heard that she was making an approach to anyone else to have Tom Nevin murdered they would go and inform Tom and deal with her and whoever she got in contact with. That was the last I heard from Tom or Catherine Nevin for a couple of years.'

When giving a deposition in the District Court in 1997, and again during Catherine's trial, Gerry Heapes described the first time Catherine asked him to murder Tom. This information had not been contained in his original statement because, he said, he had been locked up for forty-eight hours and just wanted to get everything over with. He also said that it probably didn't occur to him because he didn't think she was serious at the time. 'I don't want to look like a male chauvinist, but I thought it was just a woman in one of her moods going off her head.'

Heapes said he was up in a pool hall in Finglas and she came up to him and they went to The Barry House for a drink. She had a short and he had a glass of 7-up. For the first twenty minutes, Catherine just ranted about how she was 'getting hard done by off Tom. She was getting beaten up. She had no money. She couldn't go anywhere. He was watching her all the time. She couldn't go out. She couldn't have friends.' Then she got to the point. 'She said she was getting a terrible life off Tom, that he was bashing her up and wouldn't give her any money, and, you know, the whole lot and would I be interested in killing him ... basically I thought it was a joke, you know what I mean?' Heapes told her he'd think about it, to come back to him later.

In the Central Criminal Court, Paddy McEntee SC asked him: 'Why didn't you just say to her sorry for your trouble but as to killing him it's out of the question? You shouldn't be thinking like so, you should be talking to a marriage counsellor. Why didn't you say: I'm no longer in the IRA, I don't kill people, the IRA would never touch this sort of killing?' Heapes replied that Catherine had 'never mentioned the IRA'. McEntee asked Heapes why he had left Catherine with an invitation. Heapes replied: 'To you it's an invitation, to me it was an escape.'

Catherine had kept coming back. She knew where to find him – hanging around outside The Barry House where he grew up, or doing security for Dunnes, a shop at the side of the pub, 'keeping the kids from robbing'. 'Couldn't you say: I can't, I'm working? Why did you go with her?' Paddy McEntee SC asked. Heapes said his own motivation for repeatedly entertaining Catherine's requests was 'curiosity'. He would go with Catherine in her car and let her present the latest plan to him. Heapes told the District Court: 'The way it basically worked was she could only get the car when Tom wasn't using it. So if Tom was going to Dublin on a Monday with the take, she would have the car on a Tuesday so she would pick me up in the car on a Tuesday … She said that there would be £10,000 up front. He had to be killed. He wasn't to be robbed. He was to be killed.'

He went on to describe the various scenarios she had planned for the murder and which she outlined to him – at the house where he collected rents, at the pub where he would watch the car.

Heapes told McEntee he had relayed the message to two men, Redser and Mickser, in the pool hall in Finglas, who had a word with Catherine. Heapes said he couldn't give the men's surnames as he didn't know them. He said he understood these men had warded her off.

But he did call into Jack White's again some years later. Once when he was put out of his house by his wife and was sleeping in a portacabin where he was doing security for a firm that made toilet rolls. Heapes said he knew Tom had property and he went down to Jack White's to try and get a cheap bedsit. The next time he went down was to 'con her out of a few bob'. Catherine came in after collecting two workers from the station and insisted they stay for a meal. 'She was just telling us about some Guards that had either, I don't know, I can't remember whether it was assaulted her or assaulted her staff.'

Although Catherine Nevin denied all of Heapes's claims, most of his evidence was corroborated, including his remark about the alleged assault by two gardaí, which he could only have known about if told by Catherine.

In her directions to the jury, Judge Mella Carroll said it was not necessary that they believe everything witnesses said in order to support a conviction for soliciting to murder. She told them they could 'pick and choose' from the evidence of the witnesses, accepting it in whole or in part. The witnesses were presented as they were 'with all their faults,' she said.

THE MURDER

Reconstruction

COUNTDOWN

Come hell or high water, Catherine had to keep her husband from getting to the bank on Friday, 15 March 1996, so any accomplice could collect his payment after Tom's murder. The result was that in their last days together, Catherine could not have seemed like a more caring wife.

On Friday morning she told Tom not to worry about collecting the bags of coins for the weekend change, and she herself went to the Allied Irish Bank in Wicklow. This was unusual – Catherine never collected the coinage as she hated queues and the weight of the bags. While there, she asked the manager, John Slattery, about the latest time a person could make a lodgement. Knowing Tom, she knew that he would be able to get to the bank even if she stalled him until 4.00pm. The manager told her 4.30pm. He didn't recognise Catherine; he was used to dealing with her husband.

At 12 noon she again gave Tom some help, offering to go to Clonmahon in Bunclody, County Wexford, to collect meat. Catherine never went there – she hated the 36.5-mile drive and the weight of the packages. But today, Catherine arrived at Slaney Meats at 1.00pm and left at 1.08pm. The drive back took approximately 52 minutes and Catherine stopped off in Toss Byrne's for a coffee just before she got home.

By Friday afternoon, Tom was starting to get anxious about lodging the day's takings, some £4,500, in the bank, and this time Catherine could not get him to agree to let her do it for him. So she complained about her eyes acting up. She said that she had run out of the cream she needed for a condition which made her eyes stream in bright light. She told Tom she would come with him to Wicklow and get a repeat prescription. She rang Dr Pippett's practice before 3.00pm and made an appointment.

At 3.45pm she left Tom outside the practice and told him to wait, that she wouldn't be a minute. When she came out he was still waiting – but there was now no chance of him making it to the bank before closing time. She reassured him that the money would be safe at home until after bank-holiday Monday.

On Monday, 19 March, her behaviour was more erratic. At 8.00am, Bernie Fleming opened up Jack White's to serve breakfasts from 8.00am to 10.00am. At 8.30am, the cleaner, Janey Murphy, arrived. By 11.00am, the rest of the staff were in: Celia McDonald, who worked in the kitchen, sister and brother Catherine and Brendan McGraynor, Liz Hudson, Jessica Hunter, Debbie Killeen, Paula Fleming, Thomas Killen, Damien Power, Fiona and Deirdre Lawlor and Josephine O'Connell. At 12 noon, Catherine Nevin came down and had her hair done in the salon by Janice Breen.

The pub was very busy, serving drink and meals to the passing trade travelling to Brittas Bay on the bank holiday. At 2.30pm, Tom came down and started working in the pub.

Catherine concentrated on the lounge. But she was finding it difficult to act normally. When Catherine McGraynor asked could she stay the night in the pub after going to the Tunnel nightclub in Arklow, which the staff always did on bank-holiday Mondays, Catherine said, 'Nobody, and I mean nobody, is staying tonight.'

At 6.00pm, Catherine got a phone call from Agnes Phelan,

who lives in Avoca and whose daughter Janessa was due to work in the pub that night. Agnes rang from Lil Doyle's pub to tell Catherine that Janessa had the 'flu and wouldn't be able to come in. Catherine snapped at her too. In her evidence, Agnes said that Catherine told her she didn't believe Janessa was sick and she said she knew all about Agnes's problems with her husband's drinking. 'You need to get him sorted out, like I'm going to get fucking Tom Nevin sorted out,' Catherine said.

That evening, it wasn't just Catherine's mood that was suspicious. At around 6.00pm, Bernie Fleming was serving behind the counter in the lounge when a man carrying a bag and wearing a long black coat entered. He ordered a coffee and sat there, drinking it. He made a phone call and whispered into the phone.

At 9.00pm, Catherine told Liz Hudson that nobody was staying after the disco, end of story. Normal practice in the pub seemed to have been knocked out of kilter. Catherine paid Celia McDonald and the two Lawlor sisters their wages by cheque – this had never happened before and was a huge inconvenience, given that the banks were closed.

By night-time, Catherine had still not snapped out of it. She told Bernie Fleming to draw the restaurant curtains at 9.50pm. The curtains were never drawn; there were dark streaks on the parts of the material that had never seen daylight. Bernie's boyfriend, Jim Fagan, was at the bar. Jim Fagan thought it unusual for Catherine to clear the tables and close the front door as early as she did.

At 11.00pm, Catherine told Liz Hudson she was going out to the washing machine in the stores to check a wash, though Catherine didn't actually do any wash. She came back, saying there were fifteen minutes more left on the cycle. She told Liz not to bother ordering the vegetables until the morning, which Liz thought unusual.

By closing time, Bernie Fleming noticed that Catherine

had put on lots of jewellery. A customer, Marie Doyle, admired her Spanish bracelet.

At 12.05am the staff were all waiting in the car park to go to a disco. They had ordered a taxi. Liz Hudson tried to call the taxi firm a second time to find out what was keeping it. Liz was drinking with her husband Cecil and the Avoca Sergeant Dominic McElligott at the bar. The taxi driver, Sean Casey, arrived five minutes later.

At the same time, Tom offered to drive two customers, Frankie Whelan and Johnny Brennan, home. Catherine said she'd do it – which was unheard of – but Tom put his foot down and drove them himself. He didn't know what she was up to, but he didn't like it.

Dominic McElligott was still on the premises. He had already had two pints, but Catherine insisted he have a brandy. He declined her offer of another and left at 12.25am.

Tom Nevin's journey to both men's homes and back again was just over seven miles. The drive should have taken him fifteen minutes. He would have been home just after the sergeant left. He poured himself a glass of Guinness and went into the kitchen to do the accounts. The last till reading was at 12.56am.

Some time between 12.25am and 4.45am, when Tom was shot dead, the reason for Catherine's behaviour became clear.

Reconstruction

IN THE DRESSING ROOM

An hour before her husband's killer was due, Catherine Nevin had a brainwave. She went up to her bedroom and stooped down to lift her jewellery box up off the floor of her wardrobe. It was hidden behind her pairs of black criss-cross strapped shoes and the cardboard spirits boxes filled with summer clothes. Catherine told staff members that the outfits, packed away for continental holidays, were daubed with invisible, indelible ink that could not be washed off human hands – she didn't trust anybody. She fed them the story to keep their hands off her things when she wasn't around. When it came to her jewellery, anybody who knew Catherine knew exactly how much it meant to her. It reminded her of just how far she had come from the corrugated-iron roofed cottage that could only be entered with a bowed head, next to the Nurney Agricultural Machinery (NAM) plant in Kildare.

She sat on her bed, opened the box and ran her scarlet fingernails across her favourite treasures. First she hung her gold crucifix around her neck, then some other gifts from admirers, including her 24-carat T-chain, and the necklace with white gold gilded along its ribbed links. She draped her gate bracelet across her right wrist, and fastened the clasps of two other plain, loop-linked bracelets alongside. For her left arm she chose a detailed gold filigree wristlet to hang beside her navy-faced gold watch. She eyed her earlobe in the mirror on the back of the jewellery box lid as she tucked in her latest pair of gold-loop earrings. For her fingers she selected her most expensive sovereign ring for the right hand and placed her emerald with the marcasite petal borders beside her wedding ring on her left. She then placed rings on the rest of her fingers. The wedding ring was the one she had claimed for on insurance, but tonight everything must make her look like the loving wife. When the ceremony was finished she put the jewellery box back in its hiding place on the wardrobe floor.

The last-minute adornment may have been an exuberance on her part, time-wise, but the early hours of 19 March 1996 had been a long time coming. She wanted to add as many touches to her story as possible. She wanted to savour all other trimmings. Catherine was still replaying in her mind the moment, two days earlier, when Paul Harte had walked through the doors of Jack White's, unbidden. Back in 1986, when the Nevins bought Jack White's, they were told it was being sold because of a burglary that had taken place. Harte was the man convicted for the crime. He had robbed the previous owners, the Doyles, at gunpoint and locked them in the storeroom. A gun had been placed to their grandchildren's heads and the warning shouted: 'The money or their brains.' But on Thursday, 14 March 1996, Harte walked into the pub again. This time he was on his way down to Wicklow to visit his friend, Jennifer Guinness's kidnapper John Cunningham – a close associate of Veronica Guerin's sworn enemy John Gilligan.

Catherine could not get over Paul Harte arriving in the pub. To her, it was like a sign. The robbery he'd carried out had been her inspiration for the past seven years. This robbery was the reason she would estimate the amount robbed from the pub on the night of the murder at £16,550 –

almost the exact amount robbed ten years previously when Harte and two others had broken into the pub on a bank-holiday weekend. Harte was the only one sentenced to prison for his part in the robbery and Catherine made sure her husband and the staff knew he was free again – in the course of the murder investigation, Catherine's attempt to implicate Harte was unsuccessful.

As she closed the wardrobe door, she ran her hand down her long mink coat, a gift from Tom at a time when he still cared. Thinking of that time, she could almost hear the tune that played when the lid of an antique table in the centre of her bedroom was lifted. Tom had given her the table on their honeymoon in Rome. Like their marriage, it was long since broken. On it sat her favourite mock eighteenth-century porcelain doll with long straggling blond hair. The doll's steady clear-blue gaze eyed all who entered. Catherine would lie the doll down on its back to make its eyes close whenever she had a gentleman caller. Men must have loved the girlishness of the gesture. If Catherine had bothered to open the table top that night, for old times' sake, she might have remembered that there was a mobile panic button to trigger the pub's alarm still inside it. But then, if she had just told gardaí that she shot Tom Nevin herself, she might – given all her previous claims about him beating her – have got away with murder.

She went downstairs to make her entrance. This night had been a long time coming. And she had cast herself in the lead part. It was important to be ready.

12

THE MURDER

Tom Nevin, the fifty-four-year-old joint proprietor of Jack White's Inn, Brittas Bay, County Wicklow, was shot to death at point-blank range in the kitchen of his pub in the early hours of Tuesday, 19 March 1996. The post-mortem on the publican's body was conducted by Dr John Harbison later the same day. From the evidence provided by the position and state of the body, Dr Harbison concluded that Tom Nevin had been taken by surprise – there were no signs of a struggle. Before he slipped into unconsciousness, Tom might have been aware of his wife of twenty years putting his glasses back on his face.

But other aspects of the night in question proved less easy for Catherine to stage-manage. The guards arrived at the murder scene at 4.45am, when a squad car attached to Arklow Garda station responded to the activation of the pub's internal alarm system. Garda Martin McAndrew and Garda Paul Cummiskey, rostered for night duty, first scanned the car park of the Wicklow pub to see if there were any suspicious cars at the scene.

They then drove to the front of the pub and stopped at the door leading to the private part of the premises, which was about six inches ajar. The light was on in the hallway and as soon as the men got out of the car, they could hear moaning from inside.

They found Catherine Nevin standing in the hallway behind the door. Her mouth was gagged with a pair of nylon stockings, tied loosely around her head. Her arms were bound at the wrists, behind her back, with a blue dressing-gown belt and two braided GAA headbands – one maroon and white, and one blue and yellow (the Galway and Tipperary colours).

When she saw the guards enter, Catherine slumped into the corner of the door. Garda McAndrew reached to remove the gag from her mouth. It fell away easily, and a pair of black panties stuffed in her mouth slipped out.

The guards asked Catherine what had happened. She muttered that 'a man with a knife and a hood over his head' had burst into her bedroom for her jewellery. Then she asked, 'Where's Tom?'

Garda McAndrew removed the dressing-gown belt, but was unable to get the other cords off until his colleague, Garda Cummiskey, got a knife.

Catherine Nevin complained that her shoulder was sore. Garda McAndrew touched it and she winced. The guards lifted her up and carried her into the sitting room, putting her down on the settee. Her eyes were now rolling in her head and she appeared to be in shock. Again she said in a low voice, 'Where's Tom? Where's Tom?' Then Catherine said, 'Dominic was here – Dominic is gone.' She was referring to the Avoca Sergeant Dominic McElligott, the last customer drinking on the premises.

Catherine Nevin complained about the cold. Garda Cummiskey got a jacket and put it around her shoulders.

Garda McAndrew went upstairs and searched the bedrooms to see if anybody were hiding there. He found a portable television upturned on the landing floor, and the light on in Catherine Nevin's bedroom on the first floor, which was very untidy. He moved downstairs to carry out the same check and saw a trail of jewellery leading from the hall into the lounge towards the bar. The light was on behind the bar and the door into the kitchen was open. Even from a distance, Garda McAndrew could see Tom Nevin lying on his back at one end of the kitchen. His right shoulder was just 2ft from the door of the fridge, his right arm was outstretched and a pen was perched in his hand. The cork-tiled surface on the kitchen floor was covered in a pool of blood. Lying on the floor beside Tom Nevin was a high stool, its square cushioned seat had broken off with the impact of the fall.

Garda McAndrew knew Tom Nevin. He went over and felt to see if there were any sign of a pulse. There was none. Tom's hand felt cold to touch. The guard could see a gaping wound on the right side of his chest. McAndrew, based in Arklow since 1981, attends refresher courses in the use of fire-arms three times a year; he got a smell of gas in the room, but not gunpowder.

Garda McAndrew went out and checked the entrances and exits on the ground floor for signs of interference, to see where the raiders had entered. But he could find none. He left Garda Cummiskey with Catherine, and set off on a quick drive in the squad car, circling within a half-mile radius of the pub, to see if he could find Tom Nevin's black Omega, which was not outside the building. But he didn't see it.

By 5.40am, Detective Garda Jim McCawl and Detective Garda Joe Collins, both attached to Arklow, were on the scene. There before them was Superintendent Jeremiah P. Flynn, of Gorey station, Gardas Cummiskey, McAndrew and O'Donovan. Doctor Nick Buggle was also there with an ambulance crew.

Catherine Nevin gave the guards an account of what had happened. She said she had gone to bed at around 12.30am and was woken by two raiders who burst into her room, shouting 'Where's the fucking jewellery?' and 'Fucking kill ya.' One of them held her down, pushed her face into the pillow and pressed his knee into her back as he bound her wrists, then her ankles, then trussed them both together. His accent was 'more local than Dublin,' she said.

The other man ransacked the room, she could see something woollen over his face and he had a knife, she claimed. He was throwing things around the room and asking where was the jewellery. She said she told him it was in the press. She said she heard a noise like a saucepan dropping downstairs and a loud shout. She heard two cars drive off. When they were gone, Catherine said she had managed to free her ankles and get loose. She did not know how long she had struggled. But as soon as she freed herself she went downstairs and pressed the panic button in the hall. She did not think of calling out to her husband, or looking for him, she said.

The guards noted that while they could see red marks on her wrists, there were no marks on her ankles. Nor did they find any other binding in her bedroom.

At 12.55pm on the same day, Detective Sergeant Fergus O'Brien and Detective Garda Joe Collins told Catherine Nevin they needed to make a written statement outlining what she had already told them earlier that morning. She said: 'Joe, I gave you a statement today. I'm sitting her since 5am this morning. I will make no statement or sign anything. I want a guarantee from a superior officer and not the Superintendent, because I don't trust him that my statement won't turn up on the desk in Arklow to have it doctored the same as the other statement. I don't trust anybody in Arklow Garda Station, present company excluded.' Detective Garda Collins told her that he had only taken notes and that they needed the statement to try and apprehend her husband's killers. Catherine replied, 'I will make no statement or sign anything, it's dangerous to sign a statement, I know.'

Notes of her version of events were taken by Superintendent Flynn, Detective Garda McCawl and Detective Garda

Collins. At 5.40am, Detective Garda Collins recorded Catherine's first version of events: 'Dominic left the same time as the bus – 12 o'clock … It took only a couple of minutes – he just tied me up so quick. I heard somebody else throwing everything around in the bedroom, but I didn't see anybody except the fellow who tied me up. I was terrified. I thought he was going to kill me. He woke me up out of my sleep. I don't know how long I was asleep when he woke me up. I want to see Tom before I go to hospital. He's not dead, he's not, I know he's not. I want to talk to him.'

At 5.50am, Superintendent Jeremiah P. Flynn took further notes from Catherine. He recorded: 'The front door was open when I came downstairs. I tried to catch my nails in it to open it but I couldn't. It wasn't fully open. Just barely. He went to the bank on Friday. I went to Dr Pippett that day. Did you see him? Did he suffer? Why did they do it if they got the money?'

At 5.55am, Superintendent Flynn left and Detective Garda Collins continued the note-taking. Catherine said:

'I don't know how much cash was there – I did the daily take only. None of the staff stay late on a Sunday night ... Alan is in hospital and Tom would not give the key to anybody else. On Bank Holiday weekends they don't go out on the Sunday night they go out on the Monday night instead and they don't come back to stay ... The man in the bedroom had a knife – he said where is the fucking jewellery. He held my head down on the pillow – then I heard a loud noise like a big saucepan dropping ... I don't know how they got in. I let Dominic out – he was last out ... Tom drove Johnny Brennan home ... I was tied up for a long time. My ankles were tied to my hands for a long time. I got the legs free. I got the receiver off the phone and tried to dial 999. The lights were off. The door was slightly ajar and light shining ... Bernie and Liz have keys to the hall door ... Tom locked the bar door ... It was around 12 midnight when Tom drove Johnny Brennan home ... After the disco bus left, Liz would have locked up the back door. I went to bed when Dominic left. I was in bed by half twelve ... I am the license holder of the gun, it's up in the rafters of the store. I hid it in my bedroom and Tom thought it was too dangerous and he brought it downstairs. I have cartridges in my bedroom and Tom has some ... Tom always kept the keys of the car in his pocket ... Tom always has a wallet – he never has less than £500 in it ... Tom bought a new washing machine from Redmonds ... Two cars or something pulled off from the front after I was tied up ... It seemed an ordinary accent – not a Dublin accent. He seemed big, aggressive. I thought he was going to kill me. He put something to my back. I just saw a blade – a small blade. He tied me up in the bed. Never looked for money – about £400 in my handbag ... Tom says he was followed from Rathnew on several occasions coming from the Cash and Carry, Musgrave's and flats. Would have £1,500 in cash coming from Dublin. Car driving up near him and then pulling back. Was followed four Monday nights out of seven, the most recent one last Monday night – would be closing time. I spoke to Fintan Fanning about it two Sundays ago ... Rang looking for Pat Carroll and told Tom Kennedy. He said he would tell John Casstles ... Tom had no drink taken ... Trouble with someone in Mayfield Road SCR, Mountshannon SCR. Tom told Eileen Godkin that he was being followed.'

Detective Garda Collins stopped taking notes at 8.00am.

Reconstruction

THE SUIT

In the run-up to Tom Nevin's funeral, the local undertaker, Billy Breen, who is married to the local postmistress, Mary Breen, was having as many problems as a result of Catherine Nevin's activities as his wife had had four years previously. Mary was the one who had alerted gardaí to a letter presumably written by Catherine Nevin, ostensibly written by 'Mary Duffy'. On the day of Tom Nevin's funeral in 1996, the grieving widow was again up to her old tricks – causing mayhem. This time it was over the suit in which Tom was laid out.

She had not even noticed the suit until she heard it had been picked out of Tom's wardrobe by the bane of her life: Detective Garda Jim McCawl. Now she was creating havoc in a setting normally characterised by hushed voices and a sense of calm.

She said that Tom had hated the suit they had put him in. She said he would never have chosen it for himself. Tom was very set in his ways. He always wore a shirt, tie and jumper in the bar when serving. When he got up in the morning he would come down wearing his jacket, but he would immediately leave it out in the storeroom. He would always put his jacket on when going out somewhere, like driving the staff or customers home. He would take it off again when he came back in except if it was cold in the kitchen. When he was doing the lodgement, he would leave it on. That was the way he should be laid out, Catherine said, with a shirt, tie, jumper and his jacket, not in a suit he hated.

There was no way out of it. Billy Breen had to take the suit off Tom's body and hand it back to Catherine. To show just how strongly she felt about a suit being picked for him by Jim McCawl, she burned it.

But the show wasn't over. The guards, who had preserved the scene of the murder in order to gather as many forensic clues as possible, were about to release the place back to her, so she could organise Tom's funeral. But when Catherine saw them mopping up Tom's blood off the kitchen floor she went wild. She wanted the blood left exactly as it had spilled – so her guests would fully appreciate the horror of what had happened and just how heinous the murder was. And when she arrived late at the funeral, she blamed the gardaí for keeping her late.

Reconstruction

A HANDSHAKE

Catherine eyed the politicians at Tom's funeral. Fine Gael's Paul McGrath had paid his respects. Tom and Catherine had helped him to canvass in an election, and she had tried to call in a favour after the murder. He flatly refused. Anyway, McGrath was based in Mullingar. Catherine needed to line up someone in Wicklow.

Labour deputy Liz McManus came up and put her arm around Catherine to console her – Liz was great at dispensing the woman's touch, but Catherine didn't want a woman. Fianna Fáil's Dick Roche signed the book of condolences, but Catherine didn't really know him.

The one politician she wanted to talk to was the one with a twenty-seven-year record as a Dáil deputy; the one whose family held the longest unbroken record for serving the same constituency – the former Labour minister and former Member of the European Parliament, Liam Kavanagh. He is also former Chair of Wicklow County Council. Catherine couldn't work out why Kavanagh, the most distinguished among them, had not yet paid her his condolences. She wanted to have a word with him. She felt it was important for him to be seen in public telling her how sorry he was. But no matter how hard she tried to catch his eye, nothing moved him. He was definitely keeping his distance in the Barndarrig church grounds.

Liam Kavanagh had learned about Tom Nevin's murder from the Mayor of Seminole in Florida, when a delegation from Wicklow County Council visited the town with which Wicklow is twinned. He hadn't yet consoled the grieving widow – because when a man goes to about 100 funerals on average per year, he gets a sixth sense about the ones that aren't quite right. As soon as he arrived, Kavanagh spotted the Special Branch lads skirting the perimeter of the church grounds. He knew them by their first names from the Dáil and from high-security functions, presidential visits and the like. For the life of him, he couldn't figure out what they were doing at a country publican's funeral. He asked them out straight and they told him that she, the grieving widow, was not all she was cracked up to be.

Instinctively, he weighed up the political fall-out. It was true that if push came to shove, Catherine Nevin could claim to know him. Kavanagh had been in Jack White's perhaps five times that he could remember. But many keen golfers who had availed of the facilities in the local golf courses ended up moving on to Jack White's.

Kavanagh had dined in Jack White's after playing a round with the local judge, Donnchadh Ó Buachalla, a good friend of the Nevins. But there are many other legal eagles who are members of Wicklow golf clubs. No big deal – lots of Dublin-based lawyers who have made it tend to end up with a holiday home in Wicklow and membership of an exclusive golf club. Kavanagh's four-ball with Judge Ó Buachalla, himself a keen golfer, was enjoyable. The judge was an affable character and a good player. The deal was that the loser would buy the meal. As it turned out, the judge had to foot the bill. There was nothing unusual in the fact that they dined in Jack White's. Catherine Nevin had come up to them that day to chat. She could be very entertaining when she turned on the charm.

Kavanagh's last meal in Jack White's was with his wife. They were with their daughter, celebrating her Leaving Certificate results, when Catherine sent over a bottle of wine on the house. Kavanagh's wife told him not to come again as she got a bad feeling from that woman.

All things considered, Kavanagh made sure not to follow the example of his colleagues and pay any personal respects.

Reconstruction

In Loving Memory

The need to have people appreciate the drama of Tom's death was the reason Catherine had the word 'murdered' inscribed on his headstone, where most people might have chosen the softer option 'killed'. Catherine justified her choice of words to staff. There was nothing soft about the way Tom had been disposed of, and if the world was offended they should try stepping into her shoes, she said.

To let people know exactly how deeply she mourned her late husband, she had commissioned highly elaborate gravestones with four sets of text to accompany a statue of the Virgin Mary and his beloved darts trophy. The words she had chosen were:

> In loving Memory of Thomas (Tom) Nevin, Jack White's Inn, Brittas Bay, who was murdered on 19 March 1996, aged 54 years. Rest in Peace.

To the right is:

> When a loved one goes,
> Those we love remain with us, for love itself lives on.
> And cherished memories never fade because a loved one's gone.
> Those we love can never be more than a thought apart.
> For as long as there is memory, they'll live on in the heart.

A marble heart stands in front with the words:

> Loved ones never go away, for in our heart they always
> stay.

And in front of that:

> Do not stand by my grave and weep.
> I am not there.
> I do not sleep.
> I am a thousand winds that blow.
> I am the diamond glints on snow.
> I am the gentle autumn rain.
> When you awaken in the morning hour.
> I am the swift uplifting rush
> Of quiet birds in circled flight.
> I am the soft stars that shine at night.
> Do not stand at my grave and cry.
> I am not there.
> I did not die.

In front of that again is a plaque with the inscription: Kneel and Pray.

Catherine also made discreet enquiries as to whether she could claim VAT back for the headstones.

Catherine prepared her funeral outfit carefully. To show people exactly how much she cared, she had Tom's face engraved as a hologram and mounted onto a gold brooch, which was nicely offset by the lapel of her black suit.

For his mass card she had chosen:

> There is a reason
> For every pain that we must bear, for every care
> There is a reason.
> For every grief that bows the head
> For every tear drop that we shed

There is a reason.
For every hurt, for every plight
For every lonely pain roth (sic) night
There is a reason.
But if we trust God as we should
All must work out for our good.
He knows the reason.

But people could see for themselves exactly how deep Catherine's feelings for Tom ran. Like when she pointed out to Detective Garda McCawl on the morning of the murder how a bunch of her panties on the radiator in the bedroom would not be there at all if staff hadn't had to wash them again, after washing them by mistake with Tom's dirty socks. Like when she arrived late for the funeral and explained that it was the guards' fault – they had left her to clean up Tom's blood herself. Like when she told the Nevin family that, on second thoughts, she wasn't going to have him buried in Galway; he would stay where he belonged, a mile from Jack White's. Like when she put an ad in the **Irish Independent** to coincide with Tom's month's mind Mass (to which she was accompanied by Inspector Tom Kennedy) thanking the Arklow gardaí.

But at Tom Nevin's funeral, everyone who knew Tom knew how far removed he was from the vista at his graveside or the sight of his second wife smelling a red rose. His family have no intention of having him exhumed. But they are in the process of having the gravestones removed.

THE INVESTIGATION AND
THE COURT CASE

13

NO REPLY

On 20 March 1996, the day of Tom Nevin's funeral, Detective Sergeant Fergus O'Brien and Detective Garda Joe Collins again interviewed Catherine Nevin with a view to getting her to make a statement about events leading up to and following the murder of her husband. She said she had been in touch with her solicitor and he informed her to cooperate, and she gave a statement. During the course of the interview, Detective Garda Brennan took swabs from Catherine Nevin's hands and face. They examined her handbag and found there was no money in it. Later she told them no jewellery was missing. 'She informed us that after she let Sergeant Dominic McElligott out through the hall door on the morning of the 19th March she pulled the door closed, she Yale-locked then she mortice-locked the door by turning the Chubb key. In her earlier statement she said Sergeant Dominic McElligott had just pulled the door after him and made no mention of mortice-locking it.'

On 21 March 1996, she told Detective Garda Collins at Jack White's that when she was trying to release herself in her bedroom after the raid she got 'a funny smell, unusual smell, thought the place was on fire and the smell went away.'

On 23 March 1996, she informed Detective Garda Collins

and Detective Sergeant O'Brien that the sum of money stolen in the raid amounted to £16,550 and not £13,000 as she had first said.

The guards asked Catherine for a Z1 reading (an end-of-night till total) from the night Tom was murdered, but she said it was not accurate. She said it did not register drink purchased after closing – the reason was that if a guard raided the pub and looked at the till roll, he would not be able to say in court that according to the till roll trading continued after closing time.

On 4 April 1996, Detective Sergeant Fergus O'Brien, Detective Garda Tom Byrne, Detective Sergeant John McElligott and Detective Garda Joe Collins met Detective Gardas Brennan and Carey of Garda headquarters ballistics section at Jack White's. Their purpose was to carry out firearms tests in the kitchen to see what could be heard or smelled from Catherine Nevin's bedroom. She authorised access to all parts of the pub except her bedroom, which she had locked. They found that a gunshot could be heard from her bedroom, and that no smell travelled outside the kitchen.

On 7 April 1996, former Inspector Tom Kennedy requested an interview with the gardaí in Wicklow station. Detective Sergeant O'Brien and Detective Garda Collins met him, and he handed in documents in relation to insurance claims for Jack White's Inn. He said Catherine Nevin had told him on 4 April 1996 about a wedding ring, which was part of an alleged theft on 4 December 1993. The guards recorded in a memo: 'He told us that Catherine Nevin told him that Tom Nevin gave her the ring on a Monday night a couple of weeks prior to the murder after returning from Dublin. She said he (Tom Nevin) had spent months looking for it and that he must have eventually got it through his criminal contacts in Dublin or from a pawnshop. Tom Kennedy then said, "It's extraordinary the bold Tom recovering it himself, it's an extraordinary story after all that length of time."'

On 12 April 1996, Detective Sergeant O'Brien and Detective Garda Joe Collins called to Jack White's pub. They recorded in their notes: 'Catherine Nevin showed us into the sitting room and went back out herself. There was an open newspaper on a table in the centre of the room. Detective Sergeant O'Brien picked up the newspaper to read it and underneath it was an open index/address/telephone book, reddish-wine colour. I had seen Catherine Nevin using this book regularly, prior to this and since this. DS O'Brien drew my attention to the name Gerry Heapes and the telephone number which appeared on the open page. DS O'Brien made a note of this in his note book. On the 18th May 1996, I was shown the same index book by DG McKenna. On examination, I noticed the name Gerry Heapes and telephone number had been scribbled over, back and front.'

On 29 April 1996, at 11.30pm, the guards interviewed Catherine Nevin and asked her if she knew a number of people, among them the name John Ferguson. She denied any knowledge. She also said, 'You'll find nothing on the phone.' She had by now got a mobile phone as she knew the pub phone was tapped.

On 17 May 1996, Jack White's Inn was searched by gardaí.

On 28 July 1996, Catherine Nevin was arrested and brought to Enniscorthy Garda station, where she was held for forty-eight hours. She refused all offers of food and she did not answer any questions.

On 29 July 1996, Catherine Nevin was interviewed at Enniscorthy Garda station. Detective Garda Joe Collins transcribed the interview:

Q: Catherine, you know why you were arrested, for being in possession of information in relation to a scheduled offence under Section 30 of the Offences Against the State Act, that is the unlawful possession of a firearm at Ballynapark, Arklow, on the 19th of March 1993, the night Tom was shot dead. Do you understand that?

A: No reply.

Q: I want to go through the night of the 18th and 19th March 1996, the night Tom was murdered. Will you go through it with us?

A: No reply.

Q: Can you explain why you pulled the curtains in the restaurant, that's the restaurant in the private part of the building?

A: No reply.

Q: The staff said you were up and down to the wash room that night. You told them you were checking a wash at one stage and you said there was another 20 minutes left on it and when one of the staff checked it a few minutes later there was no wash on at all. Can you explain that?

A: No reply.

Q: You specifically told the staff that none of them were to stay in the pub – that is to sleep there on the night of the 18th, 19th March 1996 after the disco. This they would say was most unusual, particularly when one of the staff said she would let them into the pub after the disco and you said 'nobody and I mean nobody is staying here tonight'. Can you explain that?

A: No reply.

Q: You dressed up that night and wore all your jewellery. Were you expecting somebody?

A: No reply.

Q: Was Tom Nevin back after driving the customers home before Dominic McElligott left the pub that night?

A: No reply.

Q: How can you explain that your jewellery box, which was found in the lounge after the shooting, had no fingerprints only yours on it?

A: No reply.

Q: Where did the keys of the front door go – that's the hall door. You told us you Chubb-locked that door before you went to bed and hung the keys up in the hall, but prior to telling us that you told us you just pushed the door and the Yale lock latched closed. That was, you said, when Dominic McElligott left. Will you please tell us the truth about those keys?

A: No reply.

Q: You told us that when you freed yourself and came downstairs the door was slightly open and you tried to catch your nails in it to open it, but you were unable. We did an experiment with the hands behind the back and it was very easy to open it and when the guards arrived the door was open a few inches. Why did you not open the door and go out onto the roadway as you told us you wanted to do?

A: No reply.

Q: You said you were trying to untie your ankles for a long time, yet there were no marks on your ankles. Can you explain that?

A: No reply.

Q: You said to members of the Nevin family that you were reading the newspaper when the raiders came into your bedroom. You told them that, [on] the morning of the 20.03.1996 [the day of Tom's funeral] and when they asked you if you got a look at the raiders you said it was dark, the light was off. How could you read the newspaper with the light off?

A: No reply.

Q: You told us when you freed yourself you came down to the hall door, pressed the panic button and waited for the guards to arrive, and you never looked for Tom Nevin or shouted for help from him. Why was that?

A: No reply.

Q: How were you able to open the ties on your ankles with your hands tied behind your back, and you weren't able to open the hall door and that was already a few inches open?

A: No reply.

Q: Weren't you the only person who said Tom had been followed? Did Tom actually tell anybody himself that he had been followed?

A: No reply.

Q: Do you know Pat Russell?

A: No reply.

Q: Do you know Gerry Heapes?

A: No reply.

Q: Did you go to a man sometime and ask him to stage a robbery where Tom would be shot dead?

A: No reply.

Q: A man giving the name of John Ferguson rang Jack White's pub on several occasions looking for you. On 29.4.1996, DS O'Brien and I asked you if you knew a John Ferguson and you said you did not. We now know who John Ferguson is. Why did you not tell us the truth when we asked you?

A: No reply.

Q: Will you tell us about the murder – the truth?

A: No reply.

Q: Are you a member of the Provisional IRA?

A: No reply.

Q: Are you a member of Provisional SF?

A: No reply.

Q: What type of relationship did you and Tom have?

A: No reply.

Q: Was Tom assaulting you?

A: No reply.

At 10.50am the notes were read to Catherine Nevin and she was asked if they were correct. She made no reply. She was asked if she would like to sign the notes. She made no reply. The notes were put in front of her and she was asked to sign them. She made no reply or attempt to sign them.

On 16 September 1996, the gardaí discovered that Tom Nevin had taken out a life assurance policy worth over £70,000 with Irish Progressive Life Assurance Ltd.

On 4 December 1996, Detective Sergeant Fergus O'Brien and Detective Garda Joe Collins went to Jack White's Inn at 7.20pm. They asked could they speak to her in private, but she said they could speak in the presence of Tom Kennedy. Then they said that two men had made statements claiming she had solicited them to murder her husband. She told the two guards to contact her solicitor.

✦ ✦ ✦

On 14 April 1997, within thirteen months of Tom's death, Catherine Nevin was charged with his murder and with conspiring to have him murdered.

14

Catherine's 'Suspects'

Ten times after Tom was murdered, Catherine had given gardaí false new leads. All her 'prime suspects' had something in common – simply that they were innocent victims of her wild charges. Among the cast singled out for her false allegations were: a former chef; a dissatisfied tenant; a bed-and-breakfast guest; two 'cultured knackers'; a customer allegedly spiking drink with the date rape drug Rohypnol; an amusement arcade owner; an angel dust dealer; 'Dubs on the roof'; and even Tom himself.

The day after Tom's murder, Catherine reported that he had been followed, when returning from the bank in Dublin, four times in the previous seven weeks. In court, Garda Patrick Carroll of Wicklow Garda station said that he had been asked by Inspector Tom Kennedy to monitor Tom's journey. Garda Carroll described how he had waited for Tom Nevin at the Beehive pub on the N11 and had followed Tom home during the week of 19–25 February 1996. He said he saw nothing suspicious.

Next, Catherine informed the guards of an attempted break-in at the pub sometime in November 1995. She said the alarm had gone off between 4.00am and 4.15am, but every time she reset it, it went off again – five times in all. She saw a torch shining in the top landing window. She said she could see from the alarm panel that the problem was in the conservatory. She said she then got her shotgun and stood up on a chair and put the gun out through the conservatory window. She shouted that she had a gun and could hear the sound of feet running along the gravel. She said she went to the restaurant and looked out the window and saw the heads of three people leaving in a chocolate-coloured Renault 12. She didn't report this incident, she said. The alarm company's records showed that a false alarm message had been recorded at Jack White's at the time.

Catherine went on to make false allegations against a former B&B guest, who, she said, had 'cased out' the kitchen, where Tom was murdered, just before his death. Her way of describing this man and his companion during the trial contrasted sharply with the image of herself that she tried to project throughout, which was one of 'composed graciousness' and 'composed vulnerability'. This man was called to give evidence during the trial, and he was nothing like Catherine's description of him. She described him as:

'... having a moustache, and being an athletic tennis-type build, he was 5ft 10in, he was a real ladies' man, a spoofer, he had a cultured Dublin accent, about 30 years of age, money was no object, he seemed to have plenty of it. She was drinking brandy and port, he was drinking pints of Budweiser. He was a heavy drinker, but didn't get drunk. He said he owned a hair salon. I thought he was a bit of a liar. The woman he was with was about 30, she was well preserved. She was 5ft 1in in height, 5ft 2in maybe, she was well-endowed. She had a lot of make-up plastered on. She was neatly but not expensively dressed. She looked like someone who was on a limited budget. They didn't pair off as being married. He spoke to me about Tom, asking, "Houses going well in Dublin, does Tom still go up on Monday?" He said he had stayed here [at Jack White's] before. He did not, as I would have remembered him. He was lying about that. He made reference to my birthday cards. He was being over-familiar with me, which wasn't right. I don't know how he would know about Tom's business. I found it a bit strange, but it might not be unusual for someone to know someone who knows Tom. The woman was bottle blonde... after he had breakfast he brought his dishes, two plates, into the kitchen. I took the plates from him.'

The woman Catherine slated is, in fact, the man's wife.

In his evidence, the man said Catherine had refused him an advance bed-and-breakfast booking for the weekend of Tom's murder – a fact that Catherine had not mentioned during her spurious allegations. Catherine had told both him and another person who telephoned that Jack White's was booked out.

But, according to Catherine, this customer wasn't the only one who got into the kitchen under false pretences. She alleged that, two weeks before the murder, two men had entered the scene of the crime. 'They said they were looking for the johns, meaning the toilets. I told them where they were. They didn't go to the toilet. They walked up the corridor through the bar and out onto the roadway. I didn't see them after that until about five or six days later.' She described them as follows: 'No. 1: early 20s, slightly cultured knacker, fast strides, ginger-haired, cut short, curly. He was about average height. No. 2: I can't remember exactly what he looked like. He might have had a 'tache. One of them said, "Sorry, Ma'am." I would say they were both knackers. By this I mean itinerants.'

Catherine also said that Tom 'was worried' about Paul Harte, the man who had carried out a robbery on Jack White's when it was owned by their predecessors, the Doyles. Always she left something for detectives to uncover – in this case she let them find out that Paul Harte had indeed been in the pub. But the detectives were satisfied that he had nothing whatsoever to do with the Tom's murder.

If Tom had been worried about Paul Harte, he did not mention it to anybody except Catherine. Harte's visit to Jack White's took place months after Tom had a new time-lock safe installed.

On 25 March, Catherine, who had at first refused to make a statement or sign any interview notes, was again volunteering more suspects for gardaí. She told Detective Sergeant Fergus O'Brien and Detective Garda Joe Collins that a man had stayed in Jack White's on the Monday prior to the murder. She said he 'pretended to be putrid drunk' and spiked a young girl's drink with some kind of substance. Catherine claimed he got into the bed and had sex with the girl. But when Catherine returned to this story at a later stage, she seemed only able to remember part of what she had already said. This time she claimed that she herself was the one who had deliberately spiked his drink to get information 'for the gardaí' about drug activity in the area.

If the cast for her drama was growing, so was the intrigue. Catherine's false allegations were getting ever more outrageous. She said she believed there was an enemy within Jack White's. She said her passport, driving licence, Tom Nevin's passport, which had an American visa, were missing. She told Detective Sergeant Fergus O'Brien and Detective Garda Joe Collins that the documents had been in the safe with Tom's annulment papers, which were also missing.

On 29 April 1996, she elaborated. Catherine claimed that £2,000 had been robbed from a cash box during the raid. She said that she felt some past member of the staff had given out information to the raiders about the layout of the place and Tom's routine. When asked by the gardaí did she suspect anybody, she named a former member of staff. The garda memo goes on to record the level of Catherine's animosity towards the woman in question: 'She said [the woman] was one of the most intelligent people to ever work there, and was very cunning. She alleges that [the woman] stole Vodka and cigarettes on an ongoing basis … She also suspected that it was she who "stole her jewellery"!!!' The exclamation marks in the garda memo recording Catherine's claims say it all – she had already admitted that no jewellery had been stolen in the raid.

Gardaí asked Catherine if she knew someone called John Ferguson – the alias she created for financial consultant Pat Russell, to be used whenever he rang the pub. Staff had told them about the way Catherine instructed them to get her, wherever she was, if this man rang and never to take a message or hand the phone to somebody else. If John Ferguson was on the line, a member of staff would have to hold the receiver until Catherine arrived to take it from them. But instead of answering the gardaí's question as to who John Ferguson was, Catherine tried to change the subject. She pulled another false suspect out of the hat, this time an amusement arcade owner in partnership with a man she falsely claimed was an angel dust trader. She claimed the two men wanted to buy Jack White's, but she had refused to sell. Perhaps Tom was killed so they could force her to sell up, she intimated.

She created another blind alley. Gardaí notes recorded: 'She then went on to talk about a "Rave" party that was supposed to be held in [a local man's] field. She says that she gave information to gardaí and there were a lot of gardaí on checkpoints in the area. She says there was a fellow in charge of the security and he was "a wrong one". She said she had his name somewhere. She looked through her book briefly and then closed it again. When pressed for the name she again avoided the subject.'

In between lining up 'suspects', Catherine's interest in the investigation did not sound like an innocent widow desperate for her husband's killers to be caught. Gardaí noted: 'Catherine says that Tom Kennedy said to Catherine that … if [the murder] wasn't solved in the first few weeks it was unlikely to be. She asked if she was the main suspect, the No.

1 suspect in the case.'

On 4 May 1996, Catherine rang Wicklow Garda station at 9.30am and had a conversation with Detective Sergeant Fergus O'Brien. Strange things were happening at Jack White's, Catherine said. The conversation was recorded as follows: 'Catherine Nevin says that the satellite dish for Sky Sports has been stolen off the roof of the pub at Jack White's Inn. She says it's a big thing and expensive. She wants to know if it was there when the scene of the murder was searched? She says that they discovered it [was gone] when the customers in the bar couldn't get the telly working for some sports event. They went to check the satellite dish and discovered it was gone. All that was left was the bracket. It has been there for the last five years. She says that this is very unusual. She says that only the Dubs would take something like this. She says "Dubs are only into sport, sex, drink and cigarettes." She says "No-one local would take it, they wouldn't have it in them to take it." She went on to name locals who were "into illegal cards".'

She also portrayed herself as the innocent victim. According to garda notes: 'She says the Nevins have employed private investigators ... Catherine says that she is getting hassled from Galway. She says Tom's family are conducting their own investigation ... They are going over the top. Catherine says she was with the solicitor yesterday when Tom's will was read. She says that she knows what they're trying to do. They are going to politicians and making their own phone calls. She says "I am now their top target".' [Tom Nevin actually died intestate, according to the Probate Office. Catherine was clearly afraid of losing her entitlements.]

After the contents of the phone call in the morning, gardaí believed she was beginning to crack and paid her a visit. Catherine's paranoia had indeed gone into overdrive. They recorded the conversation as follows: 'She says that Tom died intestate. She says Tom made a will but as it was made before they were married it was now invalid. She says she has now to take out a bond to carry out the business until the inquest is finalised. She says she will have to take out letters of administration to his estate. She says her solicitor told her that the Nevins have engaged a good solicitor and he is asking all the right questions regarding the property, will, etc. Mr McEntee told her that the line of questions being asked by the Nevins would indicate that the Nevins' line of thinking is that if she was implicated in the murder she would lose all rights of succession and the property would go to the Nevins as next of kin. She said she heard that the Nevins had employed a private investigator to dig up the dirt on her. She then said "I had nothing to do with Tom's murder." She said that over the years she had stuck by Tom Nevin through thick and thin and she used to visit him every day when he was in St John of God's (by this she was implying that she was Tom Nevin's most loyal friend).'

But she wasn't finished adding to her production yet. She reminded gardaí of Tom's 'shady past': 'She said that after the Crimeline programme she took it upon herself to contact an old acquaintance of Tom's in the Barn (Dolphin's Barn). She describes this person as a "young grandfather" who used to be "a tea-leaf himself" but has given up crime now, but who'd still have contact with the underworld. She said she also made contact with another person with similar qualifications. She said she offered these persons substantial reward only to be payable on the appearance of a person in court for the murder of Tom Nevin, irrespective of whether they are convicted or not.' She then said she knew that her phone was tapped.

But she just couldn't help constantly insisting that her part be the leading one: 'She told us that she wanted to tell us something before we found out ourselves in case we got the wrong idea, as she knew we had been enquiring about this in the past. She withdrew money from a deposit A/C in the name of Catherine Scully, at Lr Drumcondra Road. As she wanted personally to pay for her husband's funeral. She said that on the advice of her accountant she was going to pay for the funeral out of the business account as she would be liable to tax relief on this expense. As a result she said she would be re-depositing the money into this deposit A/C in the near future. She was telling us this in case we got the wrong idea as to what the money was used for.

'She said that where there's a blade of grass there's a Nevin, they're a shower of grabbers. She said "I don't care about Jack White's. If the Nevins want it they can have it. I have enough of my own money without it. I have my own bank accounts and investments – not in Drumcondra Road." She said the Nevins were also enquiring if June (Tom's first wife) had any claim on the business.'

She rang the Wicklow gardaí again on 31 May 1996 and told them she had to talk to them about another suspect. 'She was wondering who to talk to. She asked Tom Kennedy as she values his opinion above anyone else in the world. She trusts him. She says she has been talking to a friend of hers, a valued friend of 25 years duration, a true Dub. The people of the Barn are disgusted with what happened to Tom (Nevin). Tom Kennedy advised her to talk to me. She said not to bring anyone from Arklow. She hated the guards in Arklow. They searched her home and she now feels "more violated" by the gardaí than the raiders who murdered Tom. If they wanted information all they had to do was ask.

'Catherine said she has heard that a member of staff is cooperating with gardaí in implicating her. So she tries to offset the damage. First she informs gardaí that she has had the locks on the door changed and bullet-proof patio doors fitted. She said the member of staff was hanging around with very shady people and had a set of keys to the pub. She said she herself had employed a private investigator to find out information leading to the conviction of Tom's murder, a substantial reward has been put out but would not say how much.

The PI has been working on the case since two weeks after the murder. The PI has found that information is not forthcoming.' The guards went on to note, 'Catherine puts her finger to her lips and shakes her head.'

Catherine's last suspect was her husband himself. Tom Nevin's underworld connections had been a theme before, but this time she went into detail. On 19 April 1996, Catherine stated that in December 1993 her wedding ring and some other jewellery were stolen. She said Tom 'vowed' he would get it back. 'If Tom was late coming home from Dublin on the Monday nights he would say, "I was trying to do something about the wedding ring". He never discussed it further with me. He did mention pawnbrokers shops. He also mentioned a late-night auction room or pawnbroker's on the Quays … On the Monday night, before St Valentine's Day this year, which I now know was 12 February 1996, Tom came back from Dublin late. He gave me a ring, it was identical to my stolen wedding ring. I asked him if he had got another one made. He said, "No, that is the one I gave you twenty years ago." He just said, "There it is, wear it now, I said I would get it back for you." She said Tom never discussed it any further how he got the jewellery back.'

15

ERRORS IN THE PLOT

Within hours of Tom's murder, Catherine made two remarks to gardaí who were preserving the scene of the crime, which transformed her from the apparent victim of a botched robbery into a suspect for her husband's murder.

The first slip occurred less than an hour after she had activated the pub's alarm. Catherine was asked by Detective Garda Jim McCawl and Detective Garda Joe Collins to estimate the amount of cash the intruders had stolen. Her reply was that 'the amount was in the books.' Now, there was only one way that Catherine could have known that Tom had totalled the takings for the bank-holiday weekend and had finished the accounts when he was shot: she had to have seen the books for herself. This meant that she had been lying when she claimed she had not been in the kitchen where Tom's body lay. But at 5.40am on 19 March, Catherine was still sticking to her story – that she did not believe Tom was dead. 'I want to see Tom before I go to the hospital. I want to talk to him,' she said.

She made a second comment to investigators in the immediate aftermath of the murder, which, when combined with the first, is 'damning', according to the Book of Evidence. Catherine claimed that as the raiders were tying her up she heard 'someone shouting' downstairs and 'a noise like a saucepan dropping'. But if a raider had shouted downstairs, why did all the forensic evidence suggest that Tom, who was found with his glasses on his nose and his pen still in his hand, had been taken completely by surprise? If, on the other hand, it was Tom who had shouted in an effort to alert his wife, why had he made no effort to press the mobile panic button in the kitchen where he was working? And if she had heard a shout first, how could Catherine have been asleep, as she claimed, when the raiders burst into her room? And, critically, if Catherine could hear a shout from her bedroom, how had she not heard the blast of the shotgun? Forensic experiments would show that a gun blast in the kitchen was indeed audible from Catherine's bedroom, but sounded nothing like 'a saucepan dropping'. She had once again been tripped up, as she would be so many times in the course of the investigation, by her inclination to embellish a lie. On the one hand, her ability to spin a story had maintained her reign of terror for ten years; on the other, her husband had been murdered. Now every throw-away remark she made would be analysed with microscopic intensity.

At Tom's funeral, she again put her foot in it. This time she remarked to Assistant Commissioner Jim McHugh that the smell of incense in the church reminded her of the smell she got from the kitchen on the morning of the murder. But the type of gunpowder discharged from the cartridge that killed Tom is known as nitrocellulose or cordite – a smokeless explosive. There is very little discharge, let alone odour. What can be detected bears absolutely no similarity to incense. Detectives carried out further controlled tests to see how far the smell of the shot carried. It did not leave the kitchen.

Catherine's motive, the Book of Evidence states, was 'the best known there is – greed'. Catherine Nevin stood to become a millionairess on her husband's death. She would benefit from two insurance policies, assume complete control of the business and become an 'independent, wealthy, single woman'.

The ill will she bore her husband was indisputable. Catherine despised Tom. She told Donnacha Long, who fitted carpets in Jack White's the week before the murder, that Tom was 'a queer' and that she was going to 'have him done'.

Catherine's own step-aunt, Patricia Flood, told gardaí that at Christmas in 1994, when Tom visited her, he said he 'was afraid of Catherine'. Tom also told Flood that he couldn't leave Catherine because she wouldn't let him. She wouldn't settle for half the business; she wanted it all.

According to cleaner Janey Murphy, Catherine had a terrible fight with Tom over his refusal to let her buy him out. He told her to 'fuck off wherever she wanted, he was not going to sell.' The timing of the fight coincided with what she told financial consultant Pat Russell. She told Russell that she wanted to buy Tom out, but that he didn't want to sell.

From Catherine's point of view the marriage was irredeemably over. Elaine Butler worked in Jack White's from June to July 1995. Catherine told her she was 'no longer married to Tom'. Sinead McDonald worked and lived in the pub from June to August 1994. She said the couple's arguments were heated. She woke up one night to hear the pair 'screaming at each other'.

In the last year of their marriage, Catherine bore all the hallmarks of a woman no longer able to keep a lid on her frustrations. Her behaviour was more agitated than ever. She was lashing out. In a statement to the gardaí, Michelle Lynch, who worked in the pub from June to July 1995, recalled Tom having stitches in his head. She said she understood that 'Catherine had been involved'. On 12 October 1995, an ambulance crew arrived at Jack White's and Catherine took them to Tom's bedroom. He told them he had fallen and injured his back. It was never established how he had received the injuries. For the second time in four months,

Tom required medical attention for injuries he had suffered on the premises. His wife seems to have finally succeeding in grinding him down, and he was a beaten man, in every way. Catherine's violent streak had not only been directed at Tom: Elaine McDonagh, who worked in Jack White's during school holidays in 1990 and 1991, recalls Catherine throwing a knife at her in a fit of rage.

Very little got in Catherine Nevin's way when she wanted something. In a statement to the gardaí, Fiona Lawlor, who worked in the pub, said that Catherine had told her 'she was a bitch and proud of it.' And her extramarital affairs were well known. Caroline Strahan, who worked in the pub between 1992 and 1994, testified in court that she believed Catherine had an affair with Inspector Tom Kennedy. She saw them in bed together: 'The inspector had no shirt on,' she said. Adrienne Fisher worked in Jack White's for about four months in 1993. In one statement, she said that Catherine told her she had a boyfriend in the North whom she visited every three weeks.

The conclusion in the Book of Evidence was that a case could be made against Catherine Nevin based on a combination of the overwhelming amount of circumstantial evidence and the direct evidence of John Jones, Gerry Heapes and Willie McClean. The men were traced following a search of Jack White's Inn on 18 May 1996, during which scraps of paper with a car registration and phone numbers and a personal phone directory were seized.

If the men's backgrounds were dubious, Catherine was hardly likely to approach 'scout masters' with her requests, said the Prosecution in court, explaining why the men had not come forward to the guards of their own accord. There was corroborating evidence to support their stories.

John Jones correctly placed his meeting with Catherine in the advice centre in 1989. Jones was correct in fixing 1986 as the date when the Nevins moved to Jack White's. And he claimed that on one of the occasions when Catherine asked him to get someone to murder Tom, she had black eyes. Detectives found that Catherine did have an eyelift, on 6 September 1991, which would cause a blackening of the eyes similar to bruising.

Jones also said that Catherine suggested Tom could be hit when he was doing his banking, which concurred with the accounts given by the two other men she solicited, Gerry Heapes and Willie McClean.

Jones claimed he rang a Sinn Féin colleague to tell him about her solicitations, and this was confirmed by financial consultant Pat Russell, who said he was the man in question.

It also appeared that the former IRA man, Gerry Heapes, was telling the truth. Heapes's name and number were seen in Catherine's personal phone directory on 12 April 1996 by Detective Sergeant Fergus O'Brien and Detective Garda Joe Collins. When the book was seized on 18 May 1996, Catherine had scribbled the name out.

Heapes claimed he had informed 'certain people' of Catherine's solicitations. The Garda investigation found he had indeed reported back to the Finglas cumann of Sinn Féin. Heapes was correct in claiming that Catherine had been driving a white car at the time – records show that she was driving a white Opel Kadett during the period in question. And there was only one way Heapes could have known about the double insurance policy on Tom's life – from Catherine. Heapes also said that Catherine said she could finance the hit by 'skimming money' out of the company account and into one she would set up in her maiden name, which is what happened. Catherine did open an account in her maiden name on 23 June 1989, and began to make lodgements. Heapes's claim that she took him to the flats on South Circular Road was right in terms of the address. The Nevins did have property at Mayfield Road in Rialto and Mountshannon Road, both off the South Circular Road. Heapes also said that Catherine showed him a view of Islandbridge, from where you could see Tom's car approaching – in order to time his arrival. Tom's handyman, Billy Randles, confirmed to guards that this was the exact route taken by Tom on Mondays when he did his rounds, collecting rent and making lodgements, in Dublin. Randles also confirmed that Tom would go to the Grasshopper pub for lunch, another place Heapes said Catherine proposed Tom be shot. It was only from information given to him by Catherine that Heapes could have known that Tom travelled to Blanchardstown and to Keepak in Clonee on Mondays.

The evidence of Catherine's former lover, Willie McClean, could also be corroborated. McClean said that Catherine rang him from St Vincent's Private Hospital in Dublin in 1990. Detectives found that she was in a private room in St Vincent's in October 1990 and February 1991. McClean said Catherine had offered to pay £20,000 for the hit, which is the sum mentioned by both Heapes and Jones.

Catherine had cried wolf once too often. One by one the investigators had scotched all of her claims. In the course of the interview they also got her to admit that none of her jewellery had been stolen, despite the fact that she claimed the raiders burst into her room shouting, 'Fucking jewellery, fucking kill ya.'

Catherine stated: 'I have been shown jewellery now by Detective Garda Joe Collins. I have looked at it. I identify it as being my jewellery and my jewellery box. This is the jewellery that was in the press of my bedroom. There appears to be no jewellery missing except two Sovereigns and a gold 9ct ring with light garnets circulating (sic) a diamond. These could still be in the house. There is also a wishbone ring and a blue stone with three diamonds on either side of it not in the box either. Again this could be somewhere in the house. Some time ago, within the last year, maybe July, the first two weeks, whilst the wall in Tom's bedroom was being replastered, some jewellery was found inside a loose brick. This was regarded as old Spanish jewellery believed to be 150 years old. There were two bracelets, a neck chain and a brooch. That jewellery isn't stolen.'

When gardaí interviewed the man who had replastered the pub for the Nevins, he said he had found no Spanish jewellery during his labour or heard that anybody else had.

Catherine was also dropping repeated hints about the last man on the premises. She told Assistant Commissioner Jim McHugh repeatedly that Dominic (Sergeant Dominic McElligott, Avoca) had been the last to leave the pub. She told staff member Liz Hudson that when she went to bed, Tom and Dominic were in the lounge together – although she had earlier stated that she had closed the door after McElligott left. Catherine's attempt to set him up as a suspect was rubbished by McElligott, who stated that he left before Tom came back to the pub after dropping customers Frankie Whelan and Johnny Brennan home.

The truth was that it was Catherine's own behaviour in the run-up to and over the course of the bank-holiday weekend that was suspicious. A set of keys was missing. She told Janessa Phelan weeks before the murder and Catherine McGraynor on the night of the murder that they could not come back and stay in the pub after the disco – this had not happened before. She paid Deirdre and Fiona Lawlor their wages by cheque – which had never happened before. Her delaying tactics kept Tom from getting to the bank, ensuring a maximum amount of cash was on the premises that night. She made excuses to go in and out of the storeroom, pretending to see to a wash that she had not put on. She even had the curtains in the old restaurant pulled at 9.50pm, although this had never before been done. Everything about her behaviour on the night of the murder suggested that she knew exactly what was coming.

There was hard evidence from the findings of the forensic

scientists. There was no evidence of a break-in. The scene of the attack in Catherine's bedroom did not back up the story of a woman who had been trussed up – ankles and wrists bound to each other behind her back, Mafia style. There were no marks on her ankles to indicate that they had been tied. The phone lines had not been ripped from the wall. The pillows were stacked against her headboard as if she had been reading, but there was no imprint of a head shoved with force into a pillow. The covers on the bed were not tossed and did not support her suggestion that she had struggled for 'a long time'. There was a newspaper on the bed, which was not crumpled, and a glass of scotch and 7-Up on the floor beside the bed, which, amazingly, had not been knocked over during the raid, despite her claims that one intruder was 'throwing everything around in the bedroom'. The dresser drawers, which had been emptied, appeared to have been simply upturned on the ground. The fingerprints taken from the drawers were of surgical or leather gloves, but there were no similar prints on the jewellery box – only Catherine's. The jewellery, for which she claimed the raiders screamed at her and she understood to be the purpose of the raid, was scattered like a trail from her bedroom to the front door – but not stolen. The dumping on the landing of the portable television, seized from her room, did not look like the work of a professional thief, heavily armed, with over £16,000 in takings. And then, Tom had not even had time to drop his pen, let alone put his hands up when he was shot, so why had Catherine been spared? The type of weapon used to kill Tom is a hunting weapon, used to kill game at large distances. The forensic evidence led to one conclusion: whoever called to Jack White's on 18/19 March 1996, had only one intention – murder.

Catherine's reaction was not consistent with someone who had been taken by surprise. The hours from 12.25am to 4.45am simply could not be accounted for. Catherine had not pressed either of the panic buttons in the bedroom and she was found at a 4.45am inside the house with the front door partially opened, without ever having tried to run out onto the road to get help. She claimed that it had not occurred to her to go and look for Tom or to call out for him. The only reason she would not have called out to him – the only other person on the premises who could have helped her – was her knowledge that he was already dead.

Everything suggested that Catherine had constructed the scene and selected the main characters. She gave herself a leading part, but every time she told her story there were inconsistencies. She said the bedroom light was off, but it was found to be on; she said the raider had a long knife, then it was short; he wore a hood, then something woollen over his face. She told Tom's family she had been reading when the raiders burst in, but she told gardaí she had been asleep.

The investigation examined Catherine's credibility in the past. A heavy shadow hung over her integrity, given her number of false insurance claims. As she had perjured herself in the Larry D'Arcy case, neither was she considered an honest person. There were instances too of her being capable of very long-drawn-out, calculated plotting. Could her allegations against Gardas Mick Murphy and Vincent Whelan, even at an early stage, have been designed to later back-up her allegation that she had been 'stitched-up'? She had certainly laid other groundwork. The patient who met Tom Nevin in March 1993, while both were being treated for alcoholism in St John of God's Hospital in Dublin, said Tom did not believe he had a drink problem. If it is true that Tom agreed to enter St John of God's only to get Catherine off his back, there seems to be only one reason why she was so insistent that he get treatment. It was now five years since she had first tried to get him killed. In branding him an alcoholic, she was corroborating one of the main planks of her defence.

The analysis of the information in the Book of Evidence

persuaded the Director of Public Prosecutions that Catherine Nevin did indeed have a case to answer and returned in favour of prosecution.

16

A FEMALE WALTER MITTY

Long before she would have to stand trial for her husband's murder, Catherine Nevin had cast herself in the role of victim. There were seven other Garda investigation files on matters connected with her. In all of them, Catherine took centre stage in her favourite role: femme fatale. As usual, the drama always descended to the level of pantomime. None of the files could be included in the Book of Evidence because in strict legal terms they had nothing to do with the murder case itself. But in human terms the conclusion is unmistakable – in the case of six of the seven files Catherine Nevin showed herself to be a female Walter Mitty.

File number one concerned an incident on a Monday in September 1989, when, Catherine Nevin alleged, a customer had been taken out of Jack White's at gunpoint. The day of the week is significant; most of Catherine Nevin's serious allegations described events that took place on Mondays, when she knew she would not have to persuade her husband to corroborate her story – Tom Nevin always went to Dublin on Mondays.

File number two, detailed in Chapter 3, deals with Catherine's false allegations of corruption against Garda Vincent

Whelan and corruption and sexual assault against Garda Mick Murphy.

File number three also targets the gardaí in Arklow. On 14 October 1992, Catherine made a verbal complaint to Inspector G. Griffen, but she refused to put her allegations in writing. She falsely claimed that Garda Mick Murphy was exerting influence on other gardaí in Arklow to harass members of her staff. She also said she took exception to an application by Garda Vincent Whelan seeking a print-out of alarm calls at 'her premises' – Catherine had claimed insurance for a number of robberies in the pub and the gardaí wanted the alarm records to cross-reference them with the dates of the alleged robberies.

She also queried why Garda Liam O'Gorman, Arklow, had made contact with Anthony Doyle in connection with the civil suit taken by the former barman Larry D'Arcy against her husband. It would later emerge that Catherine had paid Doyle to perjure himself in the case and to state that he, not Tom Nevin, had hit D'Arcy. Doyle later retracted this statement, saying Catherine had put him up to it for £300.

Also contained in file number three is Catherine's false allegation that Garda P. Lenigan had waited outside 'her premises' for customers to leave and then followed them. In this case, her paranoia had, in her imagination, turned a major Garda checkpoint strip on the N11 into a personal vendetta against her.

The fourth file contained an allegation that Inspector Tom Kennedy was in breach of the licensing laws on 4 December 1993. Kennedy was in Jack White's at 12.10am with another customer. The Director of Public Prosecutions directed no prosecution.

The fifth file followed a complaint lodged by Catherine on 11 April 1996. This was the date on which Catherine allowed the Crimeline crew access to the premises to film a reconstruction of Tom's murder. She got angry when the gardaí present started asking questions of her staff. She was especially annoyed that one member of her staff, Liz Hudson, had been stopped by Arklow gardaí and questioned about the whereabouts of the owners of cars parked in the car park. Catherine wrote to Sergeant Jeremiah P. Flynn:

'I would expect that this type of query be addressed to me personally. My staff have been through a very traumatic time and to witness the re-enactment of a murder scene on the occasion. This particular staff member had been working from 12 noon on the previous day and had remained on to facilitate the filming. I would also like to point out that she had been followed from our car park by the Arklow patrol car on a number of occasions at night.

'I expect that the Arklow gardaí are aware that I have a full restaurant certificate and can serve food at any time. I also do a B&B business here.

'On the night in question the only local cars in the car park that I am aware of were those of a family relative who was driving staff home and a couple of close friends who have helped me through the recent tragedy. In fact some were assisting two members of the Murder Investigation Unit – Detective Garda Tom Byrne and Bernie Hanley – who were taking statements here. I am surely entitled to have friends in the sitting room which is a private part of the house.

'I fully agree, Sergeant, that the majority of the members that you spoke about in Arklow station are decent and conscientious members. I am, however, fully determined that the actions of a few will not put me out of my home and business. We are all aware here of where the complaints that you mentioned are emanating from.

'In conclusion, I must say that at the present time I would have expected that the local Garda resources would be employed in trying to bring the callous and cold-blooded killers of my late husband to justice.'

The complaint was sent to the Garda Complaints Board, but Catherine subsequently sent a letter withdrawing her complaint.

The sixth file came about after a complaint by Catherine Nevin's solicitor, Garret Sheehan, concerning media leakage of information about the case. The letter is dated 12 December 1996, almost nine months after Tom's murder. It refers to media reports concerning the progress of the investigation, which attribute the information 'to local Garda sources'. Specifically, it concerned a report on local radio that a Wicklow woman was to be charged in connection with Tom Nevin's murder. The letter also refers to a visit by Detective Sergeant Fergus O'Brien and Detective Garda Joe Collins to Jack White's on 4 December 1996. Both matters were discontinued.

The seventh investigation file concerns a complaint by Catherine Nevin on Monday, 29 December 1997, when she phoned Wicklow Garda station at 7.29am, alleging she had been assaulted and had received a gash to her forehead. Garda Martin McAndrew went to the scene and found her intoxicated and repeating the claims. She would not make a statement. At 8.25am, Garda Duggan, Wicklow, contacted Arklow gardaí saying that he had spoken with Mrs Nevin and that she wanted to speak to Tom Kennedy. Catherine was so confused that she apparently thought Tom Kennedy was still at the station – three years after he had retired.

When Garda Martin McAndrew arrived at Jack White's, he found Catherine Nevin sitting in the lounge with the front door open. She was dressed in a pink dressing-gown, with her head in her hands, crying. She had consumed a lot of intoxicating liquor. She refused to discuss the matter, saying, 'Arklow will do nothing about it.' Garda McAndrew saw a Northern car registration on a piece of paper and radioed base. More gardaí arrived on the scene. Catherine alleged that a man had tried to rape her, but she refused to discuss the problem or to make a written complaint. There was a broken glass behind the counter.

At 11.20am, Inspector Peter Finn and Sergeant Donal Kiernan of Gorey Garda station went to Jack White's. Both men said they noted Catherine had quite an amount of drink taken. The men were shown into the dining room and, as described by Sergeant Kiernan:

'[We] waited for some time. And Mrs Nevin entered, dressed in a full-length dressing-gown. She was quite pleasant and seemed pleased to see Inspector Finn. She shook hands with him, congratulated him on his promotion and offered condolences on his recent bereavement. Inspector Finn formally introduced Garda Charlene McCormack and Mrs Nevin shook hands with her. He then introduced me and she shook hands with me. However, when I said that I was from Arklow station she immediately changed. She became hostile to us. She stated that she "wanted nothing to do with Arklow, I've said that, I don't want to make a statement, it's all right, it doesn't matter, let these two gurriers off. I don't want it to make the 8.10am news, from Arklow, like my husband's death." Looking at Inspector Finn, she said, "you know what it's like, your father died a few weeks ago, let these gurriers off." I interjected and said, "I do not discuss Garda matters outside the station and only with my authorities." She replied by asking us to go, and led the way out to the bar area. There were still a number of customers there and Mrs Nevin requested one of her staff to show the inspector "the fucking door". Again I pointed out to her that I was quite willing to take a complaint from her, deal with it quite impartially. That Arklow Garda station was the station that covered this area and that any complaint she had would be investigated. She had previously said, "it's a pity the two of us weren't killed then ye wouldn't have me to worry about." She was referring to her husband's death. She again refused to make a statement and said, "The Bull Ryan was right, ACYA – always cover your arses." In my opinion, Mrs Nevin was very drunk as there was a powerful smell of intoxicating liquor from her, unless she is a diabetic. However, I believe that she was aware of everything she said to us. At this time she returned to her private residence. I went and had a look at the alleged scene of the attack and saw some broken glass on the floor.'

Garda Charlene McCormack's observations were that Catherine 'had aired her views as to why [she wouldn't give a statement] loudly and bluntly. At this stage all three of us left the premises.'

Meanwhile, the registration number of the vehicle was tracked to Sandyford Industrial Estate in Dublin. Detective Garda Joe Collins and Garda Gerry McKenna arrived at 1.00pm to speak to the two Northern men.

Both were informed that the guards were investigating a complaint made by Catherine Nevin that she had been sexually assaulted earlier that morning. Both were cautioned that they did not have to speak, but if they did it would be taken down in writing and given in evidence. The man who stood accused answered, 'I have nothing to hide – I want to clear up the matter.'

Three times during the interview, the man told Detective Garda Collins that he felt sick from the amount of alcohol consumed the night before, and three times he went to the toilet and vomited. He told Detective Collins that he was working as a helper, delivering vehicles. He said that on Monday, 24 February 1997, while en route from Dublin to Courtown Harbour, at about 8.30pm they called into Jack White's for a meal. He said they had a couple of drinks, then decided to drop off the vehicle to the park nearby, where it was due to be delivered, and come back for a few more drinks. They decided to sleep in the cab of the truck, which had sleeping facilities. At closing time they asked for another drink and the barman, Alan McGraynor, refused them. A woman, he now knew to be Catherine Nevin, said, 'Get those boys a drink.'

She bought several more drinks for them and at about 3.30am one of them insisted on paying for a drink before he retired to the truck. But Catherine would not let him sleep outside, saying there was plenty of room upstairs.

At about 3.30am or 4.00am, one of them went to bed while the other continued drinking with Catherine Nevin in the lounge. Throughout the night she would bring the conversation around to the Troubles in the North. She put up all the drink (spirits) and told him how she had given anti-British lectures in Coleraine University. She said she had been stabbed in the back by a British soldier. She said her husband had been murdered by 'murdering druggie bastards while she was sleeping up in bed.' When the man appeared uninterested, she 'went mad,' he said, and threw a glass at him. He became frightened and ran upstairs and woke his mate, who was asleep upstairs. The question of sex never came up, he said, and he denied having sexually assaulted or touched Catherine Nevin in any way.

He handed Detective Garda Collins a set of keys, which he said he had found inside his overalls. He explained that the alarm on Catherine Nevin's car had gone off at least twice the night before and she had sent him outside with the keys to reset it. He must have put them into his pocket by mistake.

Detective Garda Gerry McKenna interviewed the man who had been sleeping upstairs and cautioned him that he was not obliged to say anything. His account corroborated his friend's story, saying that he had been woken up by his friend in the early hours.

Two staff members, Alan McGraynor and Terry Keogh, and one customer, Frankie Whelan, were interviewed in the course of the Garda investigation. They backed up the Northern men's version of events.

Meanwhile, Catherine had changed her mind and decided, on second thoughts, that she would make a statement. Garda Charlene McCormack, from Wicklow, again arrived at her home. 'When I started taking down her statement she appeared distressed but spoke freely. I did not observe any outward signs of bruising or scratches on Mrs Nevin.'

Catherine Nevin's version of events was, as ever, as colourful as it was loaded. Although she had at first told gardaí she had barely spoken to the men, she recalled a lot of detail. She alleged:

'... As I went upstairs I noticed two men sitting near the steps near the connecting door between the main pub and private quarters. I asked a member of staff if they had anything to eat. I was told they had two short grills and a pint of milk. I noticed their accents were Northern. I then went upstairs as I was wrecked. I put on the television and Crimeline came on. I remember it was about Jo Jo Dullard. This was after 9.30pm. The next thing I knew it was 10.45pm. I had fallen asleep. I went downstairs to help Terry Keogh with the last orders. I can't remember if the two men were still sitting where I had seen them. They had ordered a pint of Guinness and a pint of lager. The older of the two was driving. He was about twenty-five years of age. I think he said he was twenty-five. He had a very thin face and straight hair and I'm almost certain he said he was from Belfast. He said he left school when he was fifteen and his parents had split up. He asked me was I interested in buying drink from a friend's warehouse. I said I wasn't interested. The younger of the two ... seemed a lot more immature than the other man. He said he was attending college. There were only themselves and the staff left in the pub at this time. At this stage they asked if we do B&B. I checked and found that there were suitable rooms. We had three or four more drinks at the bar. The youngest man kept asking Alan McGraynor, a member of staff, to get the lady of the house another drink. During these drinks we had a general conversation about how the peace affected them and the difference in their areas. He said he had a deep hatred of the RUC and said many of his friends were shot. Terry left and so did Frankie at around 2.00am or 2.10am. Alan let them out. Myself and Alan talked to the lads for another hour. Alan left around 3.00am – 3.30am. He had already shown them their rooms before this. They went to bed around 3.00am or a bit before. I was worried about Alan going home in the bad weather and I asked him to stay. He was getting ready to go when the older man came down. Within a couple of minutes the older man came down. They were looking for water. Alan brought two glasses of iced water to their rooms. The younger lad asked for Southern Comfort with ice and drank it in one go. The older man asked for lager. When they had finished they want back upstairs. Alan put on his gear and left. I locked up and decided against setting the alarm with the wind as it would set it off. I had forgotten to explain to the men that if the windows were touched the alarm would go off. When I went to bed I had the light off but the television on. This was after 4.00am or thereabouts. I don't know how long I was asleep for – when I woke up it was daylight. The younger man jumped on top of me in the bed. He was fully clothed. I jumped out the opposite side of the bed. I started screaming. I grabbed the keys and came downstairs. I was terrified. I had been lying across the bed on my tummy. He just jumped straight on top of me. I was wearing a nightdress and under-wear. When I went downstairs he followed me. I went into the pub although I don't remember opening the door. I went behind the counter and he followed me. I have a recollection of him knocking over glasses. He was calling me a slut and a slag and said I needed a good dick. I think he said he had a ten-inch one. He grabbed me by the front of my nightdress. I heard a button pop. It was one of those nightdresses with buttons down the front. He picked up a bottle of spirits and started pouring it. It was a large measure and he threw it back. I was screaming at this time. His friend just appeared and started shouting at him. I don't know what he said to him.

Then they burst open the front door of the pub and got into the [vehicle], which was in the car park on the Brittas Bay road. I went out after him and they had the rig going at this stage. I jumped out of the way and took note of the reg number in my mind. As they drove by they started waving at me and laughing. I then went back inside and wrote down the number. I immediately rang Wicklow, either through 999 or direct. I gave the reg number to the gardaí. While in the bar earlier the younger man put a broken glass to my throat which he had broken. I didn't know it was 8.30am until Ann Keogh, a member of staff, arrived. It was before this, around 8.00am, that I rang Wicklow. At all times during this until they left the premises, that is from the time I was woken up by the younger man, I was in fear for my life. I wish to add that the keys to the cash box were taken. I don't know the value of the keys. I never gave anyone permission to take the keys.'

The Garda report on the investigation concluded that there should be no prosecution for the following reasons: firstly, when Catherine Nevin made her initial report to Wicklow station, her only complaint was that 'people were running amok'; secondly, she made no mention of being sexually assaulted; thirdly, she had a considerable amount of alcohol in her system and she had refused to make a written complaint until 3.00pm on 28 February; fourthly, if one of the men had robbed the keys, as Catherine Nevin had alleged, he had ample time to get rid of them. His account of the car alarm going off was backed up by staff interviewed. The staff also said that the men were not causing trouble. Finally, the men's claim that Catherine Nevin insisted that they stay was backed up by staff, who claimed the men never asked them about bed and breakfast. The Director of Public Prosecutions directed not to prosecute.

Reconstruction

CRYING FOUL!

Three separate juries were sworn in for the Nevin case after the trial had to be aborted twice. The first trial began on 12 January 2000. The public gallery was opened specially to cater for the extent of public interest in the case. A huge number of witnesses, over 170 in total, would have to be accommodated in the course of the hearing; the least they could expect would be a seat for the duration of the wait.

But sensationally, on 26 January 2000, less than two weeks after the court was convened, the trial collapsed after it was reported that the jury's deliberations could be heard from the balcony. The man who reported it was Bobby Doyle, a High Court 'crier'. A crier is much the same as a member of the tip-staff or an usher. Their function dates back to the days when paths in courthouses were cleared for judges by a cry from a man-servant or the tip of a stick. Doyle lives in Redcross about three miles from Jack White's. Like other Wicklow residents he had more than just a passing interest in the case and on several occasions watched the trial from the balcony.

He reported overhearing the jury's deliberations to the Central Criminal Court Registrar, Joe Brennan. The Registrar could not have taken Doyle's allegations more seriously. He recognised immediately the devastating implications. The jury were advised to try and keep their voices down and the Registrar asked the guard on the gallery for a second opinion. The guard pressed his ear to the fire escape door and admitted that tones, if not actual words or conversations, could just about be heard.

The Registrar had no option but to inform the Justice immediately. Judge Mella Carroll recognised the implications and took a dim view. She said she would have to discharge the court after fourteen days, on 26 January 2000. The second trial got under way, but once again things went wrong and it collapsed on 8 February, when one of the jury became ill.

Catherine could hardly believe it. When she first gave her deposition to the District Court in 1997, the court reporter described her as looking 'bemused'. She was bemused because in her own mind she had never believed that she would ever have to stand trial, she had spent too many years offsetting every eventuality that might arise after her husband had been murdered. Now it looked like her prophesy was coming to pass.

As a third trial convened, members of the jury complained about people hanging over the balcony. They found it 'intimidating'. By Thursday, 16 March, Catherine herself took ill, forcing an adjournment. There were a lot of sideshows.

At the time of going to print, the fire escape door to Court Number Four, regularly convened as the Central Criminal Court, has still not been reinforced with soundproofing.

Reconstruction

THE STATE'S EXHIBITS

As far as Catherine was concerned, the State's case against her amounted to thin air. The State Prosecutor, Peter Charleton SC, could liken her to Rose West all he liked, but the jury only had to take one look at her to see she was not a serial sex-killer, capable of mutilating young girls and burying them under the garden patio.

The comparison between Catherine Nevin of Jack White's, Ballynapark, Arklow, and Rose West of 25 Cromwell Street, Gloucester, England, was made because in both instances there was an absence of hard evidence, but there was 'similar fact' evidence. Women who had escaped the Wests said Rose was involved with her husband, Fred, in their abduction, torture and rape. In Catherine Nevin's case, Willie McClean, John Jones and Gerry Heapes all claimed she wanted Tom killed in a botched robbery over a bank-holiday weekend and that the amount paid would be around £20,000 – exactly what had happened.

But even if she were to be as demonised as Rose West, Catherine consoled herself with the fact that not one of the State's exhibits, contained in an array of clear plastic bags, amounted to actual evidence that she had killed Tom. Catherine would simply claim that the items seized during the search were planted by the guards, who had it in for her because of her allegations of corruption.

The bag labelled Number 1 contained the search warrant, dated 17/5/96 and signed by Superintendent Jeremiah P. Flynn of Gorey.

Number 2 was a prime example – a scrap of paper with John Jones's telephone number written on it. Catherine would tell the jury she had not written it and did not know who had.

Number 3 was another piece of paper seized from her bedside locker. Written on it were three car registrations – one of them led the guards to Willie McClean. She would say that whenever there was a suspicious vehicle in the car park, the procedure was to take down the number, but that she could not recall writing it down.

Number 4 was the financial consultant Pat Russell's diary, proving that their meeting had taken place in the Davenport Hotel. When asked why she made Russell use an alias – John Ferguson – when he rang the pub, Catherine would later say at the trial that she was afraid the staff would gossip if they knew she was changing accountants. She simply denied that she had refused to give the gardaí this answer in the first place, and she denied that they had ever put the question to her.

Number 5 was her own wine-coloured telephone/address book. Catherine would say that she had scribbled over Gerry Heapes's number at her husband's instruction because he was furious that Heapes had tried to get a flat from him.

Number 6 was an album of photographs containing a photo of Inspector Tom Kennedy's retirement party. Judge Donnchadh Ó Buachalla stood beside Kennedy for the presentation of two tickets to Florida. Catherine had baked the cake and organised the balloons and whole party, but what did any of it prove?

Number 7 was the till roll showing the last time Tom had totalled the takings, in the early hours of Tuesday, 19 March

1996. It proved that he had not been shot before 1.00am, but that did not mean, she would claim, that Catherine had shot him or had him shot.

Number 9 contained the stockings, tights and panties, Number 10 the wrist ties and dressing-gown belt and GAA braids with which she had been gagged and bound – which, as far as she could see, backed up her case.

Number 11 was a copy of the **Sunday Independent**, which the guards claimed they had found on her bed, unruffled by the raiders when they tied her up. But Catherine felt she had laid enough groundwork, in terms of allegations of corruption, to even make it look like the guards could have put the newspaper there themselves.

Number 12 was the blood-stained pocket lining from Tom's jacket, containing two biros. Catherine herself had given it to gardaí, claiming she found it in the kitchen. The State's case was that she could not have found it after the murder because the guards had fine-combed the preserved scene. They claimed that she must have taken it from the scene on the morning of the murder. But Catherine displayed her find like a token to relatives, claiming the guards had 'missed it'.

Number 13 was the Chubb and Yale keys found in Tom's inside pocket; Number 14 was a button found on the floor near the body; and Number 15 was Tom's wallet. All were items taken from the scene, but none of these linked Catherine to the murder.

Number 16 was a brown paper sack containing Tom's blood-stained clothes; Number 17 the blood/urine sample and head hair from the pathology tests; Number 18 contained cartridge pellets removed from his chest. All showed the circumstances in which he died – but not that Catherine had a hand in it.

Number 22 was the search warrant, issued on 26 July 1996 by Superintendent Jeremiah P. Flynn, allowing a search of Pat

Russell's premises at Merrion Square, under the Offences Against the State Act. During that search his diary, referring to meetings with Catherine Nevin and John Jones, was seized. Catherine was now prepared to admit that she had indeed met Russell, but she denied in evidence ever telling him she wanted to buy Tom out and that he would not sell.

Number 24 contained Tom's ledgers – three school copybooks and one notebook showing the pub's takings for the weekend, but not sufficient to show the price Catherine had paid for a contract killing.

Number 25 was a computer printout from the alarm company showing she had pressed the alarm button in the hall, not her bedroom. Catherine could cover that by saying that she had forgotten there were two mobile panic buttons in her room.

Number 33 was a deposit book in her maiden name, Catherine Scully, showing that Gerry Heapes was correct in claiming that she had told him she would set up an account to siphon funds. But how could they prove she had told him if she denied it? There were other ways he might have got the information.

Number 40 was her bank statements, showing her withdrawals which she had already explained to gardaí were for funeral expenses. She roundly denied that the money was a final instalment for the killer.

Catherine believed the evidence against her was pitiful and, like Rose West, that she had been demonised by the public perception of her. One of the first applications her barrister, Paddy McEntee SC, made was to stop the trial because of a 'systemised and calculated' leaking of garda material. Stories about the time gap between the estimated time of death and the delay in her contacting the guards, and the caveat entered by the Nevin family, were all designed to point the finger of blame at her. It was a grudge-motive, using public pressure to compensate for the absence of proof and to secure a prosecution. The newspapers had already cast themselves as her judge and jury, concluding that the events of 19 March 1996 bore the hallmarks of a contract killing made to look like a robbery – which was the very issue the jury had to decide.

17

SHIFTING SANDS – THE TRIAL

Judge Mella Carroll's charge to the jury deliberating case No. CC 129 of 1998, the Director of Public Prosecutions versus Catherine Nevin – 'four trials in one' – was 190 pages long. It outlined almost 100 contradictions inherent in Catherine's own direct evidence, given during her four and a half days on the stand. Catherine Nevin could have refused to take the stand, but the jury would have been able to infer an element of guilt if she had done so. In the event, the defence called two witnesses only, Catherine herself being one. The Prosecution called over 170. At forty-two days, it was the longest murder trial in Irish legal history. Catherine had refused to answer any questions put to her when detained in custody for forty-eight hours in Enniscorthy. But detectives instinctively knew she would be unable to resist taking the starring role in the drama she had constructed when it came to court. They also knew that as soon as she began to give her side of the story on the stand, the world would witness Catherine Nevin's incredible powers of fantasy. This, the investigators believed, would compensate for the absence of hard evidence. Her strategy – to issue blanket denials, using hearsay and pathological lies – had failed miserably. Before her cross-examination had even begun, Catherine knew she was hanging on by her fingernails – before the trial ended she would manage to stall the court for a week after being hospitalised on 16 March 2000. But her appearance never faltered. She sat for hours on a wooden chair with her legs crossed, holding her hands in her lap. She never changed this position and throughout stared into the middle distance with a stony expression. Her demeanour was described as one of 'composed graciousness and composed vulnerability'. But the fact remained that for Catherine Nevin to be telling the truth, twenty-four people must have conspired to tell 'barefaced lies' under oath.

Catherine's first task in the witness box was to spin a different motive from her botched robbery plot. It had been undermined because the ransacking was so obviously staged and the weapon used to kill Tom so uncompromisingly lethal. She countered the State's claim that she had Tom murdered out of 'greed and hatred' by claiming that her husband was a member of the IRA. By weaving subversives into her plot, she did not need to say why Tom was killed – it is common knowledge that the paramilitaries are a law unto themselves. The State Prosecutor, Peter Charleton SC, was taken completely by surprise, as, it seemed, was the defence. Catherine simply said that she had never told anyone before because she had made Tom a 'solemn promise'.

Having cast her husband as a Provo, she now moulded herself as the loving wife – trying to help him through his alcoholism by making sure he got plenty of sleep, and denying any extramarital affairs that might have made the jury doubt her fidelity. But in order to support her one big lie that she had not murdered Tom, Catherine needed to create hundreds of smaller ones to support what was dubbed a 'gigantic yarn' by the prosecution. However, a good liar needs a good memory and the more she spoke, the greater the number of inconsistencies in her story. Unable to keep track of everything she had said, Catherine began to double-back on earlier evidence she had given in the witness box. The prosecutor likened the changes in her story to 'shifting sands' – the ground kept moving.

Even Catherine's own barrister, Paddy McEntee SC, appeared to be taken by surprise by her 'IRA and loving wife' bombshell. The staff of Jack White's and the guards patrolling the area had already been cross-examined. McEntee had put no questions to them about IRA meetings being held in Jack White's 'once a month in winter' from 1988 on, to support his client's case.

Catherine also claimed that IRA meetings were being held in the pub in the middle of the night, and that she could hear the men arguing about money. She did not know why the staff had never heard or seen anything. She was the one who cleaned up after the men before anyone was up, she said. When asked if she believed the IRA were content to have an alcoholic as a member, she said she didn't know. She did not support the IRA herself, she said.

Her reason for never telling anybody that Tom was in the IRA was that she had made Tom a 'solemn promise'. She did not say in evidence, as her lawyer did in summing up her case, that she was afraid of retaliation.

Staff had not been challenged about their description of Tom and Catherine's marriage as a business relationship. Nor was anyone asked if they had ever seen an associate of Tom's, described by Catherine as 'tall, with a long coat, receding hair and a briefcase', who last called sometime after St Valentine's Day. Catherine claimed this man would exchange sterling with Tom, who then laundered the money through the pub.

Catherine described her husband as a 'very nice man with more good than bad qualities, a very private man.' She said that his priorities were: first, their marriage, which was happy, then business, then football, hurling and darts. Her evidence was that she had never committed adultery. Her evidence was that she could not recall whether Inspector Tom Kennedy had ever stayed at the Horse and Hound Inn, Ballinaboola, at a time when she was there unaccompanied by her husband, but it changed while she was in the stand. First she said it might have happened that they were there at the same time, then that she did not recall it happening. She was unable to corroborate her story that Tom [Nevin] had come and stayed with her in a chalet during one of her residential weeks in Ballymaloe House in Cork, because she said he didn't meet any of the other people on the course while there. Although Ballymaloe House is one of Ireland's finest restaurants, Catherine said she and Tom had not met anyone else on the course because they had eaten 'in a buffet upstairs in a pub in Midleton' because she said that Tom thought Ballymaloe House restaurant was too expensive for him.

Although she went to Puerto Rico with her husband in 1988 and Tenerife in 1989, she claimed Tom travelled alone because he needed weeks off during the year, whereas she only needed short breaks. She also said it was impossible for them to get away on holiday together because of the pub.

Catherine claimed she regularly dined out with her husband. She said they had a meal on her birthday on 28 February 1996 in Blakes Restaurant, Stillorgan, and some weeks earlier in The Courtyard in Donnybrook. But she explained these claims could not be corroborated because Tom did not use cheques or credit cards to pay and had not booked in advance.

On the one hand, she said she had had a drink with Inspector Tom Kennedy once or twice; on the other, she agreed to five or six locations where they were seen together, including Naas. She also said they had eaten together in Toss Byrne's and Lil Doyle's.

Catherine denied the evidence given by Caroline Strahan, who said she had seen Tom Kennedy in bed with Catherine and that he was not wearing a shirt. Catherine said Tom Kennedy only stayed late in the pub on rare occasions, depending on how long it took Tom Nevin to prepare a lodgement. She said Tom Kennedy was 'certainly not' ever in Jack White's after 3am (except on the night of his retirement party), but this was contradicted by the guards on duty who patrolled the area and saw the inspector's car there up to 6am on many occasions.

Catherine said that she and her husband had always had separate bedrooms from the outset of their married life because he worked late hours. But this had been contradicted in Orla Glennon's evidence earlier in the trial. She said that when she had worked in Jack White's in 1989, Tom and Catherine had shared a room – this evidence went unchallenged by Catherine's legal team. Tom Nevin's sister, Margaret, also said that the couple had shared a room when they first got married and were living in a flat off South Circular Road. Catherine had said it was a two-bedroom flat, but Tom Nevin's sister said that it had only one bedroom.

Catherine claimed her husband was fighting with his family over their father's intestacy, but this was contradicted by the family, who denied there was any problem.

Her description of her husband to Assistant Commissioner Jim McHugh on 23 March 1996 as an abusive alcoholic who drank a litre of whiskey a day, chain-smoked and hit her, was in conflict with her evidence that she had no problem with Tom's drinking. Catherine said she had 'no recollection' of making such a complaint to the Assistant Commissioner and that she had 'no idea' where he could have come up with such an idea. She said she only told him about one incident of violence, when she had ended up in St James's Hospital. She said she had never told him that she was considering separating from her husband.

Catherine claimed that she only contacted the financial consultant Pat Russell because Tom suggested it. But again this was hearsay because Tom was dead. She denied not knowing the identity of John Ferguson, the alias used by Pat

Russell when he rang the pub. She claimed she couldn't have told Detective Garda Collins, on 29 April, that she didn't know who John Ferguson was because he never asked her.

She admitted telling Pat Russell how concerned she was about Tom's drinking, but earlier she had said she had no problem with his drinking. In earlier evidence, she had said that alcoholism isn't a problem once you know how to deal with it and make sure the alcoholic gets plenty of rest. She denied ever telling Russell that Tom wasn't pulling his weight in the business. She said she never told him she wanted to buy Tom out and that he was the one who suggested using the alias 'John Ferguson' when contacting her by phone. But Russell was not challenged on his claim that Catherine told him to use the name. Catherine said Tom knew the identity of Pat Russell, but, of course, Tom was not there to back up her claim.

Catherine even tried to rewrite what had happened on the Friday before the murder, 15 March, so it looked less as if she had been deliberately trying to keep Tom from getting to the bank. She claimed she had returned from the bank by 12 noon, after collecting coins, but the evidence given by John Slattery, the bank manager who dealt with Catherine's request about the last time for lodgements, said she called after lunch. It had not been put to Slattery that he was mistaken, because Catherine was ad-libbing as she went along.

Catherine contradicted her own story about the bank, first by claiming that Tom couldn't go to the bank himself because he was busy in the kitchen as barman Alan McGraynor was in hospital and the workload was doubled. Later she said Tom couldn't go to the bank himself because he hadn't got out of bed by that time – the implication being that he was suffering from a hangover.

In trying to offset the damage of her delaying tactics, Catherine also put back the time of her appointment with Dr Pippett. She said she was back in the pub by 3pm, after calling into the chemists to collect her prescription. But Dr Pippett's receptionist claimed that Catherine only phoned to make the appointment between 1pm and 3pm. This evidence also went unchallenged by Catherine's barrister at the time.

Catherine claimed that Tom was a 'disciplined alcoholic', who only drank at night when she was in bed. When asked how, if she were in bed, she could have known that her husband was drinking, she claimed that she knew Tom was an alcoholic because he told her. But this evidence was inadmissible as hearsay. When it was put to Catherine that the staff of Jack White's said that Tom only ever sipped a glass of Guinness at night, she claimed that her husband would spike his drink with spirits. But there were no spirits in the glass of Guinness found in the kitchen beside his body.

Catherine also claimed that her husband only ever got up for work at 3pm, except on Sundays and Mondays, but the evidence of the staff was that he was always up by lunch, and they were not cross-examined at the time to corroborate Catherine's claims.

Donnacha Long, who fitted carpets in Jack White's a week before the murder, said Catherine told him that her husband 'was a queer' and that he [Tom] was having an affair with the barman, Alan McGraynor, who was pointed out to him by Catherine. Long said Catherine told him that Alan and Tom had gone on holidays together, and that Catherine said she was going to 'have Tom done'. Catherine simply denied ever having this conversation with Long. She said that Long fitted the carpets the week of the murder – when Alan McGraynor was in hospital – so she could not have shown him the barman. But it was never put to Long during his cross-examination that he got his dates wrong. Again, Catherine seemed to be making things up as she went along.

Catherine explained that she had paid the Lawlor sisters by cheque instead of giving them cash as usual because she didn't know Tom was letting them off early, at 6pm, and therefore didn't have the cash ready. But Deirdre Lawlor told the court she finished working at lunchtime, and waited around until 6pm for her sister to finish and her mother to collect them. The girls were not cross-examined as to whether Tom had let them off early. This was a further part of Catherine's ad-libbing.

Nor was it put to staff that Catherine frequently did the clothes washing and regularly asked for the restaurant curtains to be pulled, as she claimed.

Catherine also tripped herself up in falsely claiming that when Tom arrived back from dropping two customers home, Sergeant Dominic McElligott was still in the pub.

Catherine said she had not told staff they could not stay the night on the night of the disco.

Catherine had been unable to describe the two intruders she claimed burst into her room because, she said, the light was off – she always used the lamp and never the overhead light in her room. But the two guards who were first on the scene, Garda Cummiskey and Garda McAndrew, both said they found the overhead light in her bedroom was on.

When quizzed about the intruders, she claimed that she didn't say anything when they burst into her room. But in her statement she told gardaí she had spoken to them – to tell them where her jewellery was.

Her first description of the size of the knife used by the raiders to threaten her was to Detective Garda Joe Collins, when she said it was short; but on the stand she said she was sure the knife was long.

Her account of the raiders' accents also changed from 'not being a Dublin or Wicklow accent' to being a Bray accent, which is, in effect, a Wicklow accent.

Catherine said she didn't hear the banisters being broken by the portable television that the raiders apparently dumped in the landing. But it would have been impossible for her not to have heard such a crash, just as it would have been impossible for her not to hear the sound of a gunshot in the kitchen – which she again likened to a 'pot dropping on the floor'.

Catherine described how she had been sleeping on the left side of her bed because the lamp was on on the bedside locker on the left. She said she rolled over to the right and put the newspaper she had been reading on the ground before going to sleep. But the photos taken of her bedroom by Garda Vincent Flood showed the newspaper was on the bed and the covers were drawn back neatly on the left.

Catherine said she had not tried to open the front door when she freed her legs and got downstairs, but this contradicted later evidence when she said she 'tried and tried' to open the door. She told the jury that she had hidden behind the curtain of the door and stayed there until the guards came, but she had never made any mention of doing so in previous interviews with the guards. Nor had the guards who found her inside the house been asked if she had been hiding behind the curtains.

Garda McAndrew said that the stocking around her head was hanging loose, but Catherine said that he removed it. McAndrew was not challenged about his version of events.

At one point, Catherine said the belt of a dressing-gown was used to tie her ankles but this contradicted her evidence that she didn't know what was used to tie her ankles.

On the one hand, she said she had no recollection of anything being put around her shoulders, but later she said she was given a jacket by a guard.

In relation to her refusal to give a statement, she denied telling Detective Garda Collins that it was 'dangerous' to do so and Detective Garda McCawl that it would be 'doctored'. Catherine said she had no recollection of them asking her for a statement.

To back up her claims that she had been 'stitched-up' because of a grudge against her by Arklow gardaí, Catherine reduced the time span between an alleged assault on a bar girl and the reporting of the incident to nine months. In fact, she had not reported the alleged incident until two years after it was alleged to have occurred.

She claimed she had no recollection of ever saying, on the day of Tom's funeral, that she was reading before the raiders burst in – a conversation that was overheard by members of the Nevin family.

One of the reasons, Catherine told the court, she had not immediately pressed either of the two panic buttons in her bedroom was that she did not know they were there. But Detective Garda McCawl told the court that on the morning of the murder she had told him there was a panic button on the window.

Catherine said she didn't know that there was a panic button on the window ledge as she never pulled the curtains in her bedroom.

Asked why she hadn't used the panic buttons, she said that even if she had remembered that they were there, Tom didn't allow them to be used. She agreed that Tom was sensible, but she repeated that he didn't allow them to be pressed. Catherine said her husband did not want the Arklow gardaí on the premises under any circumstances.

Her claim that she had found Tom's jacket pocket after the pub was released back to her was incorrect in the time she gave. After the murder, the scene of the crime was preserved while the gardaí gathered evidence. Catherine claimed that after they had finished, she found in the kitchen a blood-stained pocket from Tom's jacket, containing three biros. But the guards were not cross-examined about Catherine's claim that the pub was released back earlier than they said. She told the jury that the guards took the pocket off her for only fifteen minutes, but Garda Yvonne Foran, on duty at the time, said they had the pocket for some time.

Catherine claimed she had a loving relationship with her

husband, but one of Jack White's workers, Janessa Phelan, and Tom Nevin's niece, Anne Marie Finnerty, claimed she had told them, separately, that she and Tom were splitting up. Catherine also denied having a conversation with Anne Marie Finnerty's mother, Nora, at a relative's month's mind Mass, about separating from Tom. The staff of Jack White's were not challenged about their claims that the couple's relationship was a business one only.

Her account of the length of time she stayed in hospital after her eyelift operation was contradicted by Dr Early. Catherine was trying to give herself more time in hospital so it would look like the bruises had healed, undermining John Jones's claim that on one occasion she had called to him with bruised eyes and said Tom had hit her.

Catherine denied ever soliciting anyone to kill Tom. She said she had never driven a white car in Gerry Heapes's presence and that she had never asked him to kill her husband. Gerry Heapes was not challenged about his claim that he attended Jack White's opening, which Catherine denied. She also said she didn't tell John Jones that her husband was beating her up and that she didn't ask him or Willie McClean to kill Tom or to have Tom killed. She agreed that Tom had died intestate and that she stood to inherit his property, but she said she never told this to Willie McClean and didn't know how he knew.

In evidence, she said there were no front door keys missing and that she had never told members of staff that Judge Donnchadh Ó Buachalla had a set of keys.

Her evidence regarding an attempted break-in at Jack White's before the murder was that the alarm was turned off at the control panel by Tom. But this was in conflict with the evidence of the alarm company, which said the customer at Jack White's had phoned to tell them it was a false alarm.

The bed-and-breakfast customer who claimed Catherine told him that her marriage was not going well, was not cross-examined to the contrary.

Although, on the one hand, she had told gardaí after the raid that no jewellery had been taken, in her evidence she said she was not now saying this, just that she had found the two sovereign rings she had been concerned about.

She was asked why Tom was concerned about the man who had robbed Jack White's ten years previously, and she said that this man knew where the safes were. But Tom had had a new time-lock safe installed, which he himself had been unable to open for two weeks after making a mistake.

She claimed Exhibit Number 5, her personal address and phone book, was a pub directory and that she crossed Gerry Heapes's number out in front of her husband because Tom was annoyed that Heapes had called earlier, when Catherine was out, looking for a flat to rent. But this contradicts what was put to Gerry Heapes when he gave evidence, which was that he was talking to Tom when Catherine arrived in.

Catherine said her eye operation took place in St Vincent's, but Dr Early said it had taken place in the Mater Hospital. She said she was certain it was in St Vincent's, but Dr Early's evidence that the operation took place on 6–8 September 1991 in the Mater Hospital had not been challenged. She said she had eyelift and liposuction in St Vincent's and a tummy-tuck in the Mater. When it was put to her that she was deliberately shifting the location to make it look as if Willie McClean had not noticed bandages on her eyes when he said she solicited him, she claimed she didn't have bandages, she had stitches that were hardly noticeable.

She said she didn't tell Detective Superintendent Fergus O'Brien or Detective Garda Joe Collins that she had hired a private investigator, a claim that had been recorded in their notes.

She said she had only taken Jones's number down because her husband had told her to. She said she had not put John Jones's number inside her locker. Asked if she were saying it was a plant, she said she didn't put it there. But when the guard had entered the piece of paper in evidence, he went unchallenged. She was asked who Harry was, the name written next to Jones's, but she said she didn't know.

Nor did she know who had written down Willie McClean's car registration number or how the scrap of paper on which it was written had gotten into her bedside locker. She claimed that her husband told her McClean was a counterfeiter, but this was never put to Willie McClean.

Her response to the allegation that she had gone to Sinn Féin in 1984/1985 asking for assistance in buying or leasing a pub premises was that her husband was in the pub business, not her.

Asked how John Jones could have known about Tom's banking arrangements, she said she didn't know. Nor did she know how Jones knew about their plans to apply for an EU grant to turn the pub into a truck-stop. She had not asked Jones up to six times to kill her husband, she said. She claimed she had never told Jones that two men who attacked her in a flat on South Circular Road were from the SAS.

She said she had never mentioned to Detective Superintendent O'Brien or Detective Garda Collins that she had turned the Mortice lock that night, which meant that the raiders could not have gotten in without a set of keys.

Asked why she hadn't gone looking for Tom once she had freed herself, considering she had heard a shout from down-stairs and he was the one person in the house who could help her, she said she didn't understand the question. Then she explained that it hadn't occurred to her because Tom always said he could look after himself. She said all she thought about was herself. She said she did not ask the first garda on the scene, 'Where's Tom?' She said she wanted to get out onto the road and get help. She said she 'tried and tried' to open the door, which the guards testified was open, in contrast with her earlier claim that she didn't try that hard. It was put to her that the reason she claimed she had amnesia covering the time she came down the stairs to the time she was found, was so that she would not have to explain why she hadn't checked to see if her husband of twenty years was all right.

Although she said she didn't hear the noise of the gunshot, tests showed it would have been audible. In her statement she said she was familiar with firearms – the gun club used the pub for three months of the year and she had her own shotgun.

It was put to Catherine that she was putting lies and hearsay in the mouth of a dead person. But as always, when Catherine was spinning a story there was a grain of truth at the core of every lie. Catherine, not Tom, was the one drawn to mix with Republican figures and was suspected of being a member of the Provisional IRA by the gardaí who arrested her. And according to staff in Jack White's, she was the one with the drink problem, not Tom Nevin.

18

A LITANY OF INJURIES

Left arm bent at the elbow, Catherine Nevin held up her hand to demonstrate to the court how she still couldn't straighten her middle finger properly. She had taken the stand at 2.50pm on Tuesday, 14 March 2000 to deny murdering her husband, and now she was informing the Central Criminal Court of her various medical complaints.

'I had to have it stitched from here to here ... I got a tetanus injection and, I'm almost certain, something for the pain as well because you could see the bone,' she explained.

She had received the injury after a man had slashed her with a shard of glass. She had put her hand up to protect her face, she said. She did not repeat in court what she had earlier told Jones – that her attackers were from the SAS – for the same reason she never told staff in Jack White's that most of her ten hospital admissions were for cosmetic surgery. The reason was that people were too quick to judge. Catherine didn't want the jury to think that she was the type of woman who knew anything about the world's most notorious army in case they concluded that she must be associated with terrorists. She needed their sympathy, not their criticism.

She applied much the same logic when it came to her medical history. A woman who has had her eyes lifted, liposuction, tummy tucked and nether regions enhanced goes through every bit as much agony as someone being repaired after a car accident. But people only feel sorry for someone in pain when it hasn't been voluntarily inflicted. So every time Catherine was admitted to 'St Vincent's Private,' she told staff in Jack White's that she was getting chemotherapy for cancer.

She felt she had enough real health problems in any case to justify the sympathy and the offers of help that flooded back as a result. For instance, in 1987 she was diagnosed with pernicious anaemia and for the first time in her life she could not be accused of overplaying the scene. She revelled in the drama of it all, administering her injections in public to convey the urgency of her condition; and she would visibly flinch at the sight of the needle in her hand, telling staff she would never get used to it, never.

Hospital admissions became as regular as annual holidays and now that she was diagnosed with a real condition, she no longer needed to justify them. She had three golden rules that kicked into play each time she felt one of her turns coming on: the first was never to join a queue in a waiting room – she would always insist on being seen immediately; the second was to always stay in a private room when in hospital; and the third was to refuse visitors. 'I tried to discourage visitors and always asked the nurse over the floor to try and say I couldn't have visitors. If you're sick in hospital, to me, visitors is the last thing you want,' she told the court. And it was perfectly reasonable: the last thing you need when you're having an operation to make you look better is someone gawking at you without your hair done or make-up on.

Anaemia was not her only complaint, she told the court. Some days her eyes would stream and she had been prescribed a specially medicated cream. The story was told with all its gory details. If she had to actually touch her eyeballs to rub cream onto them, why shouldn't people know about it? Beauty has its price, she liked to tell the girls in Jack White's.

On the Friday before St Patrick's weekend in 1996, Catherine found that her eyes were bothering her again. On that day, she found the daylight particularly bright and made Tom take her to Dr Pippett's practise to get her prescription as her eyes were watering. Although she was 'seen to very quickly', Tom didn't have time to make it to the bank and lodge the pub's takings. This time there was a very large price to pay: £16,550.

With all the talk in court about how sick she was, Catherine obviously couldn't help feeling sorry for herself. By the time her second day on the stand drew to a close, she was absolutely exhausted. Then she had an idea.

As on every other occasion when life was not going according to plan, Catherine turned the tables. She got sick. Nobody could accuse her of faking it, she thought, because she had already told the jury about her medical problems. She set about making the story a bit more convincing. At around 10.00pm, after a few drinks on her own in her ground flat at Mountshannon Road, she called to Robert Sinnott in flat 2. Sinnott is a student of sociology and pathology, and Catherine felt comfortable surrounded by medical people – flat 4 was let to Dr Adnan Al Shaufi, a Syrian doctor, and Fram Kain Ahung was in flat 5. Catherine herself was in flat 1, just inside the front door. Even she had to admit that her flat was like a hovel. All her life people had been picking up after her and she just couldn't seem to manage on her own. There were dishes stacked with half-eaten, week-old dinners, and clothes everywhere.

Robert Sinnott had lived in flat 2 since 1995. When Catherine called to his door, he let her in and gave her 'a bit of grub'. Catherine told him she worried about the names she had mentioned during the trial and said she felt at risk. With her plan corroborated, she left his flat within an hour.

The following morning she rose early, sipped some washing-up liquid and started to vomit. She may also have taken Paracetamol, which may have interfered with her medication. When her brother, Vincent, called she didn't answer the door or the phone.

They took her to St James's Hospital, where she was seen to straight away. The court was adjourned until Catherine had returned to full health. She now had six days to work on her story. It was time enough to weave in all the sub-plots – Tom's association with the IRA, the death threats against her, her own bravery.

On 20 March, she was back on the stand, in flat shoes and without make-up or nail varnish, explaining the reason for the delay. The jury were excluded from the court while the judge heard her account. In her hospital bed she must have recalled how life had taught her through bitter experience that a voluntary illness never gets the same sympathy as an accidental one, and so she said that when she got back to her flat that night 'a friend, a connection of my husband's' was waiting there for her. She had tripped over his legs.

'He was sitting on the couch. I was very frightened. He told me to sit down. He told me I was naming people I shouldn't be and causing problems and that I wasn't going to name any more people. I told him my evidence was almost complete. He told me I wasn't going to name anyone else. He made me take tablets he took out of his pocket, in a white container, a plain white container, my Lord. I don't know how many he made me take. He gave me something white to drink, it tasted like milk. I was very, very frightened. I remember getting sick, and I got sick a second time. After that I don't remember any more. I just remember my sister in hospital talking to me.' Catherine hadn't expected that she would be asked to describe the attacker, but she obliged nevertheless. 'Well, he was wearing an anorak with a hood and he had a beard. From what I can remember … he would be nearly forty years of age.'

But a good liar needs a good memory. And with all the pressure she was under, Catherine forgot that there were two guards, Detective Garda Richard Kelly and Detective Garda Kenneth Donnelly of Kevin Street, stationed at her front and back doors because she had already claimed she was getting death threats from the IRA.

And she forgot that she said the man in the anorak had forced her to take the tablets as soon as she tripped over his legs. She wouldn't have had time, therefore, to change out of her blue suit into the pink silk pyjamas she was wearing in the ambulance. And she forgot that Robert Sinnott, who spoke to her late on the night of the alleged attack, also heard her moving around at 7.00am the next morning.

In spite of all the work she had put into her story, it wasn't admitted as evidence against her; the jury were prevented from hearing it. But it made the guards protecting her uneasy. They were convinced that Catherine would pull another stunt to get the sympathy her first one had been denied. She had already tried to give them the slip in Crumlin Shopping Centre – where she always got her hair done before court and did her shopping afterwards – they found her in the fire escape.

After she failed to get her story as far as the jury's ears, the guards became convinced there would be a car crash involving Catherine. People are always sympathetic to car-crash victims.

◆　◆　◆

The jury took a record twenty-nine hours and thirty-six minutes of deliberation over five days before returning guilty verdicts on all four counts. On Tuesday, 11 April 2000, Catherine Nevin (49) was found guilty of murdering her husband, Tom (54) by a unanimous verdict. She received the mandatory life sentence. On the charge of soliciting John Jones in or about 1989 to murder her husband, she was found guilty by a majority verdict of eleven to one. On the charge of soliciting Gerry Heapes to murder Tom Nevin in 1990, the jury returned a unanimous verdict of guilty. On the charge of soliciting William McClean in 1990, Catherine was found guilty by a majority of eleven to one.

19

THE ASSASSIN

For Catherine Nevin, the lure of criminality was irresistible. It didn't matter to her what someone's affiliation was, as long as they lived according to her own guiding principle – a willingness to do whatever they had to, in order to get what they wanted. In common with subversives, drug barons and ordinary decent criminals, she had a pathological disregard for minor considerations – such as adhering to the law.

But she made a mistake if she thought she could commune with opposing factions, such as the IRA, drug dealers and gardaí, at the same time. If she had been playing with fire when she began to court the gardaí, in doing this she was adding dynamite to the heady mix.

After Tom's murder, detectives confined their investigation to three prime suspects, all linked to Catherine's double dealings. They included: Dutchy Holland, the man who described himself as the 'prime suspect' in the Veronica Guerin murder; an anti-drugs activist and former IRA man who was kicked out of the IRA for misappropriating funds; and, of course, Catherine herself.

Catherine Nevin
The Book of Evidence puts the proposition that Catherine

herself may actually have fired the shot that killed Tom herself. It is a theory that explains why Tom Nevin's body did not show the signs of a man unduly surprised by his killer's presence.

Gardaí had already established that Catherine Nevin was lying about not being in the kitchen on the morning of the murder. She knew Tom had completed the takings for the weekend when he was shot; the question now was whether she had pulled the trigger herself, or was present when someone else did.

Gardaí kept in mind that she had told Gerry Heapes, whom she solicited ten times to murder her husband, that she wanted Tom to die in her arms. She even said that she was prepared to be wounded herself in the course of the shooting.

Although her clothing was tested for residue of gunpowder, none was found. Only Catherine's night clothes were tested, but if she had shot Tom before changing for bed the evidence would not be there since her day clothes were not tested. Swabs from her hands were useless – Catherine brazenly told gardaí as they took the samples that she had 'already washed' herself.

If Catherine did shoot Tom, she needed an accomplice, someone to tie her up, and get rid of the gun and Tom's car – to build up the picture of a botched robbery. Gardaí believed it was unlikely that a professional assassin would link himself to the murder by driving away in the dead man's car. There were too many chances involved, like being stopped at a checkpoint, or something unforeseen happening – being caught in a murdered man's car was suicide. The car was found the day after the murder in Dartmouth Square, Dublin.

They gardaí concluded that Catherine's accomplice would have to have robbed Tom Nevin's Opel Omega before the murder. Tom would not have noticed that his car was stolen when he was concentrating on his accounts at the rear of the pub. The likelihood was that once the all-clear message had been conveyed from Dublin that the car had been dumped in Dublin, word could be sent back to Brittas Bay to shoot.

Catherine's action of having the curtains drawn may have been a signal to her accomplice to enter the building. Certainly her excuse to staff for disappearing into the stores – that she was doing a wash there – was proven to be untrue. This could have been the point in the night when an accomplice could have been brought into the pub – detectives found no signs of a break-in. Jessica Hunter claimed that Catherine kept going up and down to the private part of the residence before the pub closed. Was she checking to see whether her accomplice was safely hidden?

Another aspect of the theory that Catherine was in the kitchen at the time of the shooting concerns Tom's glasses being fixed on his nose. Although it was presumed that they stayed on because there was no struggle, the force with which he must have hit the ground from his perch on a high stool after being shot at point-blank range was severe. Who else if not Catherine would have put Tom's glasses back on? Who else would be interested in demonstrating this final act of power over a dying man, and who else could have shown so little remorse?

Patrick Eugene 'Dutchy' Holland

When detectives began to investigate who executed the hit on Tom Nevin, Patrick 'Dutchy' Holland (57) was almost certain to be in the frame. Holland had bought a house in 1995 in Lissadel, Brittas Bay for £30,000 cash and was in the process of doing it up. He had been seen in Jack White's talking to Catherine Nevin on several occasions. Staff remember Holland would park his motorbike outside when he dropped in, although he never drank alcohol on the premises.

Dutchy Holland is serving a twenty-year sentence in Portlaoise Prison for possessing cannabis with intent to supply, since being sentenced by the Special Criminal Court in November 1997. His former boss, John Gilligan, is to face trial for the murder of Veronica Guerin. Another member of the gang, Paul Ward, has already been sentenced for the murder.

There are indications that Catherine did solicit Dutchy Holland. In the summer of 1995 he had had a party in Jack White's. Holland's infamy would not hit the headlines until after Guerin's assassination but Catherine would have been familiar with some of his Republican paramilitary associates in the Provisional IRA and Irish National Liberation Army. Catherine stated in court that she could find out a person's criminal record by giving Inspector Tom Kennedy a few details – such as their car registration.

According to locals who had reason to do business with Holland during the renovation of his new house, he was very quiet and kept himself to himself, unlikely to befriend the likes of Catherine. But she had proved herself capable of casually telling a carpet fitter that she was going to have Tom done. And based on the evidence of two of the state's main witnesses, John Jones and Gerry Heapes, many other people seem to have known about her plot to kill her husband.

In his early days, Holland was a junior manager for Donnelly's Sausages, in Cork Street, Dublin. He lost his job after being sent to jail for six months in 1965. When he came out he forged a new career in burglary, eventually graduating to armed robbery. Gardaí caught him after a bank robbery in 1981. He admitted another robbery and was sentenced to seven years imprisonment. After his release, his activities went unnoticed for four years until he was found with seven sticks of gelignite in a flat in north inner Dublin. One of the arresting officers was Tony Hickey, now Assistant Commissioner, who spearheaded the investigation into Veronica Guerin's murder. The gelignite, detonators and fuse wire, were stolen from Arigna Mines in Leitrim and thought to have been stored for safe-breaking.

In prison Holland became a fitness fanatic and as soon as he was out, he returned to crime physically stronger and mentally more dangerous than ever. The underworld came to regard him as one of its most ruthless players.

On his release from prison in September 1994, Dutchy became involved with the gang who later plotted Veronica Guerin's murder. At first he tried to launder his drugs money, around £3,000 a week, through a legitimate front – a magazine publishing company.

Holland was one of several people whom gardaí questioned in connection with the murder of the Dublin criminal-turned-builder, Patrick Shanahan, whose hit was ordered by one of Holland's associates. As in the Guerin murder, a .357 Magnum revolver was used to kill Martin Cahill (The General). Both were shot five times.

But it was after the Cahill hit, that Dutchy rose to the top of the criminal ranks in the turf war which ensued. The casualties in the gang warfare were Michael Brady, who was shot dead in his car on Ellis Quay in September 1996, and Jimmy Redden, shot dead in a public house off Parnell Street in April 1996.

After Veronica Guerin's murder, gardaí started a very large operation centred on particular areas. Certain premises were searched, and on 1 October 1996, a set of keys was found that, according to the supergrass and state-protected witness, Charlie Bowden, opened a warehouse in Greenmount industrial estate – where huge quantities of drugs were being stashed.

Gardaí searched the unit on 6 October1996, and found 47kg of cannabis at the warehouse with an estimated street value of £470,000. They were convinced they had hit the nucleus of a drugs importation and distribution network. They discovered a number of items in the unit, including electronic weighing scales, wigs and false moustaches, sixty-seven blank driving licences and sheets of paper with nicknames and figures, including references to 'The Wig' – the nickname used by Dutchy in the gang.

Although he was never caught in actual possession of drugs, a search of his house in Brittas Bay for the firearm used to kill Veronica Guerin discovered two blank counterfeit driving licences linking him to the warehouse. Prosecutor Peter Charleton SC (who also prosecuted Catherine Nevin) made the case for the state that Holland used the warehouse as a wholesale distribution shop for dealers. Combined with the evidence of Charlie Bowden, it was enough to put him away for twenty years.

The severity of the sentence led to an outcry from legal watchdogs. Just weeks earlier, a Dublin criminal Warren Russell had been sentenced to only five years imprisonment for possessing £2.7 million-worth of cannabis. And in July 1995 an English drug smuggler caught with 700kg of cannabis, with an estimated value of £2.7 million, received a seven-year sentence. At the time of Dutchy's arrest on 9 April 1997, the Special Criminal Court was told that gardaí 'believed he had murdered Veronica Guerin.' He was also questioned about the Tom Nevin case.

But Dutchy was unlikely to have been easily manipulated by Catherine. When he believed he would be charged with the murder of Veronica Guerin he fled the country. When he returned to Ireland, he orchestrated interviews with the media deliberately to jeopardise his trial. Even during his interrogation in Lucan, he had top-of-the-range recording devices implanted in the heels of his shoes. These he planned to use as evidence, when making the case that he was stitched up.

Veronica Guerin had called to Jack White's after Tom Nevin was murdered, just weeks before she herself would meet the same fate. After her murder, the IRA put a hit on Dutchy's head. They presumed that two murders linked to the same pub within the space of three months, were no coincidence. She was accompanied by her friend, the Arklow independent counsellor Nicky Kelly, who had been cleared of involvement in the Sallins Train Robbery. Although Kelly did not know Catherine Nevin personally, Veronica Guerin hoped that his presence would make her own introduction to Catherine easier – because Catherine would recognise Kelly. But, according to Nicky Kelly, instead Catherine flew off the handle, cursing Veronica Guerin, barring her and calling her a prostitute.

On 9 April 1996, Catherine Nevin made the following written complaint about the incident to gardaí: 'Went from the sitting room to the Lounge of my premises with my Insurance agent at 3.05pm. I was approached by a female who produced an identification card and introduced herself as Veronica Guerin. She asked for an interview. I told her that she had some cheek to come into my premises after doing a scandalous and scurrilous character assassination against me, my family and my business. I informed her that I would see her in court with my legal team. I said that I would prefer to work as a prostitute than do what she did for a living. I ordered her to leave my premises and never to return. When leaving the premises she jeered at me and gave me a two-fingers sign. She left in a red car 94KE 2645.' Nicky Kelly emphatically rejected Catherine's story that Veronica gave two fingers or jeered. Less than three months after Veronica Guerin called to Jack White's Inn to interview Catherine Nevin she was assassinated while making her way back from Naas District Court where she had been summoned to appear for a traffic offence. The gang who killed her had very good information with regards to her whereabouts, her car make and registration.

To investigators, the coincidence of Dutchy's criminality and Catherine's plotting seemed too strong to ignore. But as the IRA gathered information about the whereabouts of Dutchy, he had fled the country. As gardaí investigated another suspect they inferred that it was reasonable to assume that Dutchy might have been well above Catherine Nevin's league financially. Why would he bother risking everything he had acquired to get involved in a domestic contract killing for the kind of money he could afford to burn?

The Third Suspect

A third suspect, who had previously had IRA connections, was arrested by gardaí and brought to Arklow station in September 1996, under the Offences Against the State Act. The real purpose of his arrest was to interrogate him about Tom Nevin's murder.

He is a maverick former Republican kicked out of the IRA for misappropriation of funds. He lives in Dublin and was attached to the 'deniable unit', the fundraisers of the IRA. Before this unit went on a 'mission', their IRA membership was revoked, so that if they were captured, the IRA could disclaim involvement with them truthfully. These members were highly skilled at resisting interrogation techniques.

However, he was genuinely 'stood down', having been held responsible for shortfalls between money being robbed and money being handed over. He subsequently began operating protection rackets for business people but had the IRA on his back over these 'freelance' operations.

When he was picked up by gardaí in the Brittas Bay area, he was brought in for questioning about his knowledge of IRA stashes and questioned about the Tom Nevin murder. All his IRA training came into play to frustrate the questioning.

The gardaí could not work out what he was doing in Wicklow. After the IRA washed their hands of him, he had eked out a role for himself as a self-styled chief of an army fighting the 'drugs war' in the capital. Often, communities gripped by heroin can be desperate for any kind of leader to get them out of the abyss. The technical meaning of a looped green ribbon (free Republican prisoners) is ignored in the desire to rid the streets of the walking zombies that used to be their children and call a halt to the crime sprees that support a junkie's habit.

This suspect developed a talent for whipping up a crowd to fever pitch. Presiding over kangaroo courts, he referred decisions regarding the eviction of addicts or pushers back to his audience – 'the People'. Anyone had the right to accuse a neighbour of involvement in drugs, but once named there could be no refusal to appear and answer the charges. This suspect's gavel was an iron bar. There was no reprieve. One wing of his vigilante army could be despatched in an instant to kick in doors, throw furniture over a balcony and carry the wanted man or woman to 'the People's' court, kicking and screaming. It was a desperate remedy for a deadly problem.

When challenged, this suspect seems to lose control. Decisions for which he is held personally responsible, upset him more than anything. IRA-connected figures from Dublin were involved in attacks on drug abusers in the mid-1990s.

This suspect's reputation would have been known to the Nevins when Tom worked in Dolphin's Barn in the mid-1980s, as the anti-drugs movement was beginning to emerge. The Nevins would also have encountered him at The Barry House in Finglas, amongst their Republican contacts there.

Unlike the previous men Catherine had solicited – John Jones, Gerry Heapes, Willie McClean and possibly Dutchy Holland – this suspect had the hunger for the cash. And he answered to no one.

Before Catherine Nevin came to trial, the Republican movement had never been known to allow its serving or former members to give evidence on behalf of the State. Traditionally, they were precluded from assisting the State in a prosecution in any way. But in the Catherine Nevin case they had multiple reasons for sanctioning cooperation.

Firstly, they were afraid of the assumption of 'no smoke

without fire.' Every Tom, Dick and Harry knew Catherine had solicited them to kill her husband but they did not want to be linked to the murder of Tom Nevin in any way. They are not in the business of domestic hits.

Secondly, they suspected Catherine had been supplying information to the Guards about their members beginning in 1988 when she informed on an up-and-coming member, claiming he was involved in an abduction incident in the pub.

Reconstruction

A Smile for the Cameras

Whenever she appeared in court, Catherine made sure to smile. She would flash her eyes sideways, never looking directly at the target, and smile. It was a sign of ease, a sign of innocence.

In 1993 she smiled at the Arklow gardaí in the District Court when she got an every-day early-morning licence – despite their objections. Early-morning licences enable publicans to serve alcohol from 8.00am. They are normally given only in exceptional circumstances, when events such as marts or matches are expected to attract a crowd. Jack White's did not qualify, the guards said.

Four years later, on 10 March 1997, Catherine was again smiling, this time at the cameras, as she arrived in the High Court to try and set aside the **caveat** entered by Tom's mother, Nora. 'Bab' had been trying to prevent Catherine from inheriting Tom's estate since five months after the murder. But she was an old woman and, as Catherine told the court, Catherine was the one who had managed Jack White's Inn and the Nevins had never interfered with her running of the premises. The Nevins weren't concerned about Jack White's for the moment. They had been informed that Catherine could not continue to run the pub without transferring the licence into her own name – and to do that she would have to give public notice in the newspapers. So for the moment, Tom's family concentrated on keeping his wife from selling his other property.

When Catherine applied for probate to administer Tom's estate, the Nevins reacted with proceedings. In her affidavit, Nora Nevin said: 'I say and believe the applicant remains a suspect in the murder of my son.'

In March 1997, the issue had finally come to court and Nora Nevin's barrister, Henry Burke SC, grilled Catherine about her involvement in Tom's death. He asked her what questions she was asked when detained for forty-eight hours in Enniscorthy Garda station in July 1996. Catherine replied that she didn't 'understand the implications of the question.' But she did. The implication was that she was about to lose £1.5m.

Burke asked her what answers she had given to the gardaí during the forty-eight hours. Catherine said she referred them to her statement, although the truth was she had made no reply.

Her own barrister, Barry White SC, said the question of a Garda investigation was irrelevant. Whether or not the widow might have been interviewed in the course of that investigation was immaterial.

'I am not guilty of any offence in relation to my late husband's death or any other offence whatsoever in relation to him,' Catherine said. She told the court that the joint bank account had been frozen and she had had to borrow money. It was very difficult, she said. She didn't say how much harder it was not knowing whether she would finally inherit approximately a million and a half pounds through the sale of the two houses off the South Circular Road and the sale of the pub.

Judge Shanley refused to lift the **caveat**, although he made it clear: 'She [Catherine Nevin] is entitled to her good name and a presumption of innocence. This court's refusal to clear off the **caveat** should not be seen in any way reflecting on her innocence. This court has no function in adjudicating on any allegation of a criminal kind.'

Catherine made sure to smile as she left the court.

It wasn't over yet. On 29 September 1997, despite the objections of the gardaí, the licence for Jack White's Inn was put into Catherine's sole name by Judge Donnchadh Ó Buachalla, who heard the application in chambers. There was no notice of a hearing in the newspapers. The guards were outraged and filed a report demanding action.

The following month, November 1997, Catherine was again in the local court, this time in relation to her application for the renewal of her early-opening licence, renewed every year since 1993. The application came before Judge Murrough Connellan.

The gardaí again objected on the grounds that there was no swell in the population to entitle Jack White's to such an exemption. Catherine reminded them of the nearby building site, the quarry workers, the farmers travelling to the Irish Fertiliser Industries plant, the golfers and the tourists. She sold around thirty breakfasts a day, she claimed. But Superintendent Pat Flynn, Detective Garda Paul Cummiskey and Sergeant Thomas Finnerty all said they had never witnessed this extent of trade at the pub in the mornings.

Judge Connellan refused to grant the licence. The law did not envisage passing travellers or workers on their way between jobs as the kind of trade meant by the Act.

On 11 April 2000, Catherine gave a smile for the cameras as she was led to Mountjoy – after being found guilty of her husband's murder. But Nora Nevin hadn't lived long enough to smile back at Catherine.

Epilogue

On Tuesday, 11 April 2000, Catherine Nevin was found guilty on the charge of murder and guilty on the three separate charges of soliciting to murder. Judge Mella Carroll announced: 'Your sentence for murder is obligatory and I so pronounce. You had your husband assassinated and you tried to assassinate his character as well. I hope the family of Tom Nevin can take some consolation in this verdict.'

For sixty-one days, over three trials, Catherine Nevin had sat in the Central Criminal Court as the evidence was laid out against her. Twice, her trial had been aborted. The third jury found her guilty. She was 'guilty – guilty – guilty – guilty' on all four counts.

As the verdict was announced, Catherine's stony expression changed into a wry smile. But to those in the courtroom her sense of shock was palpable. Dressed in a navy powersuit, long blond hair flowing and decked in gold jewellery, the forty-nine-year-old being led away to the prison van was an unlikely Mountjoy inmate.

In her handbag was the £200 spending money she had planned to splash out on a round of celebratory drinks for her family in the Beehive pub less than five miles from Jack White's on the N11. When the jury deliberations dragged into the weekend, she had backed Call It A Day in the Aintree Grand National. She even joked that Julia Roberts wasn't good-looking enough to play her part in the movie.

These were the outward signs of just how invincible Catherine Nevin considered herself. She believed she was literally going to get away with murder because for a decade she had managed to get away with so much. Throughout her marriage she was locked in a terrible bind with her husband. The more he put up with, it seems, the more she despised him. Towards the end of his life, Tom Nevin was both unwilling to put his elderly mother through a second marriage breakdown and afraid of leaving his second wife. Catherine came to hate the man whose ex-wife called him 'gentle giant', who was dubbed 'Daddy' by the young members of staff; and she hated him for exactly those reasons others loved him – his passivity. It was not enough for her to separate from her husband because she wouldn't settle for half the pub and property. She believed she was entitled to all of it. But when her husband was found shot through the heart on the kitchen floor, she finally felt the full wrath of the law. Murder is murder – to conspire is as criminal as pulling the trigger; to conspire is criminal even if the killing is not carried out. Tom Nevin was dead. Come hell or high water, Catherine would have to face the music. She had considered herself so untouchable. After all, she had laid the groundwork she thought would cover every eventuality – even the possibility of being charged herself.

On 7 June 2000, when Catherine Nevin was brought back to the Central Criminal Court to receive seven-year sentences on the three charges of soliciting to murder, her barrister Paddy McEntee SC argued his grounds for appeal: they included a recently received letter from the Revenue Commissioners, confirming that his client had been suspected of laundering money for the IRA. The true extent of the Black Widow's web of deceit looks set to continue to unravel for years to come.

In February 2003 Catherine Nevin's appeal hearing finally came before the courts. But, this time round, the star attraction did not take centre stage. Catherine had learned the hard way that her own highly colourful contributions to the original case were anything but helpful and she chose not to apply to attend the hearing.

Instead, she remained in Mountjoy where, in characteristic chameleon style, she had managed to adapt very well to her surroundings. For a time, her closest companion was Regina Felloni, the daughter of King Scum, Tony. But the pair fell out when Regina stashed a hypodermic needle and heroin in Catherine's cell to offset a routine search by screws. Catherine claimed to have stabbed herself with the needle and, true to form, she now demanded a transfer out of the main prison, claiming that her life was at risk due to the possibility of contracting life-threatening diseases like AIDS or Hepatitis C.

Amid much controversy, Catherine Nevin was placed in the pre-release wing, normally the reserve of prisoners reaching the end of their sentence. Here she was (and still is) entitled to privileges other prisoners can only dream of: she could cook for herself and she had the run of a self-contained house. This gave her the luxury of focusing all her energies on preparing for her appeal, her last bid for freedom.

And, even out of sight, Catherine was continuing to fire the public imagination – Celtic Bookmakers offered odds that she would win the appeal. The odds started at 3:1, then dropped to 5:4 in the build-up to the hearing – indicating that punters were backing Catherine's chances of winning.

In court, some twenty grounds for the hearing were lodged.

Catherine's barrister, Paddy McEntee SC, argued there was no way his client could have got a fair trial because of adverse media publicity and the 'systematic leaking' of information on the case by gardaí.

Secondly, he stated that each of the four charges against her – murder and three times soliciting to murder – was each so serious that four separate trials should have been held. The evidence on the murder was heard first, and had prejudiced the jury when considering the soliciting charges, he claimed.

Thirdly, the by now notorious Garda Special Branch Files, listing Jack White's for special revenue treatment, could have influenced the jury's final decision. At face value, if Jack White's was considered worth putting under Garda surveillance, this appeared to corroborate Catherine's claim that Tom was linked to the IRA. And this detail should have been disclosed to the defence by the State, McEntee argued.

And, finally, it was claimed that the judge's charge to the jury, just before Catherine's conviction, was unfair to her.

But the three appeal-court judges were not convinced and Catherine lost the hearing, which had lasted four days. It concluded that the conviction was indeed safe, and that she did not have the right to a re-trial.

In dismissing the appeal, Mr Justice Geoghegan said that while a great deal of the publicity was 'inappropriate and inexcusable' there was no real or serious risk of an unfair trial. He said there was a big difference between a one-day trial immediately after adverse publicity, and a forty-two day trial.

The fact that the solicitation charges were separated from the murder by a period of six to seven years did not preclude them from being joined together in a single trial, he maintained. All four charges were factually similar and supported the case of a conspiracy by Catherine Nevin to murder her husband, Tom, who died in the way she had plotted so many years earlier. It was 'just and convenient' to compartmentalise the charges in a single trial, as Peter Charleton SC had argued for the DPP.

The court dismissed the relevance of the Revenue document which listed Jack White's as having suspected connections to paramilitaries on the basis that the Nevins' previous pub premises had been frequented by persons with IRA connections, and this was known to the jury.

And finally, Judge Mella Carroll's directions to the jury were deemed to be 'most appropriate'. (Sadly, Judge Mella Carroll has since passed away. But even the tribute writers could not resist referring to the electric courtroom atmosphere when she faced her most notorious opponent.)

The appeal-court ruling cleared the way for Tom Nevin's brothers and sisters – Patrick, William, Mary, Nora, Margaret, Noel and Sean – to pursue the legal action which their late mother Nora had begun. Tom's estate had been frozen until the criminal charges against Catherine were disposed. But, as in every previous encounter with the Nevin family, Catherine would fight them tooth and nail. In 2004 she appealed to the Supreme Court to overturn a High Court decision which secured a caveat originally lodged by Tom Nevin's late mother, Nora, in 1997 and preventing the estate from being processed. As long as that stayed in place, Catherine could not touch the inheritance, including Tom's life insurance policy of IR£78,000 (approx €99,000), savings of IR£197,000 (€250,000), properties at Mayfield Road and Mountshannon Road, Dublin, or the IR£620,000 (€787,200) proceeds from the sale of Jack White's (all at 1997 values). The Nevin family needed the caveat in place while pursuing a case to disinherit her on the grounds that a person cannot benefit from murdering another. But the Supreme Court dismissed Catherine's appeal and the estate remains frozen.

ALSO BY NIAMH O'CONNOR

CRACKING CRIME
Jim Donovan – Forensic Detective

A fascinating look at the ground-breaking work of Dr Jim Donovan and his forensics team. Dr Donovan outlines the development of this relatively new and intriguing science. He and his scientists have been instrumental in solving some of the country's most high-profile crimes, often using the tiniest clue – a fingernail, a spatter of blood, hairs – to crack the case. But success has come at a price: Dr Donovan was the victim of a car bomb planted by Martin Cahill. But he survived and continued to track down criminals using only the weapons of science.

Send for our full-colour catalogue or check out our website